Forward

I was inspired to write this book by my ̣
myself and the lives of those around me. ..., g......... ..ope is ....at you
will use these ideas and practices in your daily life.

Thank you to all of my supporters, you are my greatest inspiration and motivation.

The Power of Stillness: Finding Balance Through Non-Action

Introduction
Chapter 1: The Essence of Stillness
Section 1
- Understanding Stillness
- The cast of consistent motion
- The Decline of Mindfulness in Modern Life
- The Rise of Distraction and Its Consequences
- The Importance of Non-Action
- The Necessity of Balance in a Fast-Paced World
- The Transformative Power of Stillness
- The Historical Significance of Stillness in Human Experience
- The Promise of Stillness in a Chaotic World

Section 2

- Exploring the Concept of Stillness
- The Interconnectedness of Mind, Body, and Spirit
- The Role of Stillness in Spiritual and Philosophical Traditions
- The Science Behind the Benefits of Stillness
- The Intersection of Stillness and Intentionality
- The Path to Embodied Presence and Awareness

Chapter 2: Nature Immersion
Section 1.
- Nature as a Teacher
- Immersing Ourselves in the Healing Power of Nature
- The Healing Power of the Outdoors
- Mindfulness Practices in Natural Settings
- The Art of Mindful Walking and Its Connection to Stillness
- Mindfulness and the Art of Stillness
- Integrating Nature-Based Practices into Daily Life
- Cultivating Stillness in Daily Life
- The Path to Authentic Living
- Creating Outdoor Rituals for Presence

Section 2

- The Practice of Wuwei
- The Philosophy of Non-Action and Its Relevance Today
- Letting Go of Control and Embracing Spontaneity
- The Connection Between Wuwei and Mindfulness
- Practicing Wuwei in Everyday Life
- The Liberating Power of Non-Action in a Busy World

Chapter 3: Intentional Living
- Defining Personal Values
- Aligning Daily Actions with Values
- The Impact of Intentional Choices on Wellbeing
- Sustainable Living and the Art of Acceptance
- The Connection Between Sustainability and Stillness
- The Importance of Gratitude and Acceptance in Sustainable Living

Chapter 4: Gratitude Practices
- Cultivating a Culture of Gratitude
- The Benefits of Gratitude on Mental and Physical Health
- Effective Strategies for Practicing Gratitude
- The Connection Between Gratitude and Acceptance
- The Concept of Amor Fati
- Daily Gratitude Exercises
- Fostering Acceptance Through Reflection
- Integrating Gratitude into Daily Life and Rituals

Chapter 5: The Philosophy of Non-Action
- An Introduction to Wuwei
- Historical Context and Relevance
- Applying Non-Action in Everyday Life

Chapter 6: Digital Detox
- The Need for Digital Disconnect
- The Impact of Technology on Our Mental and Physical Health
- Strategies for a Meaningful Digital Detox
- Creating a Healthy Relationship with Technology
- Reconnecting with the Present Moment

Chapter 7: Sustainable Living
- Principles of Sustainable Lifestyle Choices
- Harmonizing Daily Life with Nature
- Building a Community of Sustainability

Chapter 8: Eastern Philosophy Meets Western Wellness

- Bridging Philosophical Traditions
- Integrating Eastern Practices into Modern Life
- The Role of Stillness in Holistic Health

Chapter 9: Cultivating a Practice of Stillness
- Techniques for Daily Stillness
- Creating a Personal Sanctuary
- The Long-Term Benefits of Stillness

Chapter 10: Embracing Impermanence and Change
- The Impermanence of All Things and Its Connection to Stillness
- The Importance of Embracing Change and Uncertainty
- The Role of Mindfulness in Navigating Transition and Change
- The Connection Between Impermanence and Acceptance
- Finding Freedom in the Face of Change.

Chapter 11: Embracing the Journey
- The Path to Balance and
- Overcoming Challenges in
- Celebrating Progress and Growth

Chapter 12: Embodied Presence and Holistic H
- The Interconnectedness of Body, Mind, and Spirit
- The Science Behind the Benefits of Embodied Presence
- The Connection Between Embodied Presence and Self-Awareness
- The Importance of Self-Care and Self-Compassion

Conclusion

Disclaimer:

The publisher and the author make no guarantees concerning the level of success you may experience by following the advice and strategies in this book. You accept the risk that results will differ for each individual. The testimonials and examples provided in this book showcase exceptional results, which may not apply to the average reader and are not intended to guarantee that you will achieve the same or similar outcomes.

Unless otherwise indicated, all names, characters, businesses, places, events, and incidents in this book are either the product of the author's imagination or used in a fictitious manner. Any resemblance to actual persons, living or dead, or events is coincidental. All rights, including copyrights and trademarks, to this content remain the exclusive property of their respective owners. This material is provided for informational and educational purposes only. No representation or warranty, express or implied, is made regarding the information's completeness, accuracy, reliability, or suitability.

Introduction

In an era of constant busyness and the omnipresent allure of distractions, the pursuit of stillness may appear countercultural. Nevertheless, as we navigate through the clamor of contemporary life—juggling responsibilities, rushing from one obligation to another, and experiencing a constant digital connection that often leaves us feeling profoundly isolated—it becomes increasingly evident that the practice of stillness is not merely a luxury but a vital pathway to achieving balance, mindfulness, and authenticity.

This book invites us to delve deep into the essence of stillness and its remarkable transformative potential. We will embark on an enlightening journey exploring the interconnected realms of mind, body, and spirit by weaving together ancient wisdom and modern insights. We will uncover how embracing non-action can catalyze significant personal growth, fostering a state of serenity and clarity.

Each chapter is designed to illuminate various dimensions of stillness. We will explore its historical significance, examining how cultures have revered the practice of stillness to cultivate inner peace.

The relationship between stillness and nature will be a crucial focus, highlighting how immersing ourselves in the natural world can enhance our capacity for reflection and rejuvenation. Furthermore, we will delve into the philosophy of non-action, illustrating how letting go of the constant need to do so can lead to profound insights and revelations.

Additionally, we will investigate the integration of gratitude and intentional living into our daily routines. Each section will offer practical strategies and reflective exercises to help you cultivate a culture of appreciation, emphasizing the importance of recognizing and appreciating the small moments that often go unnoticed. We will also tackle the concept of impermanence, encouraging you to embrace change and uncertainty as integral parts of the human experience.

As we navigate the impact of technology on our lives, this book will provide tools to redefine our relationship with digital devices and the natural world. By immersing yourself in the healing power of stillness, you will discover how to move through life with greater ease, grace, and purpose. This journey is not simply about finding moments of pause amid a hectic world; it is about reclaiming your authentic essence and aligning your daily existence with your most profound values.

Whether you aspire to slow down from the relentless pace of life, seek more profound connections with others, or strive for a more meaningful and fulfilling existence, the philosophies and practices outlined within these pages will serve as your guide. Together, we will embark on this transformative journey toward finding balance through stillness, ultimately leading you to a life that is not only more intentional but also profoundly enriched. Welcome to a path that invites you to experience peace even amid the chaos, fostering a presence that will enhance your daily encounters and interactions.

Chapter 1

The Essence of Stillness

Understanding Stillness

Understanding stillness is a multifaceted concept that transcends mere physical inactivity. It encompasses a state of being wherein the mind, body, and spirit align harmoniously, allowing for deeper awareness and appreciation of the present moment.

In a world that often glorifies constant motion and productivity, embracing stillness can seem counterintuitive, especially for fiercely independent and driven people. However, this chapter seeks to illuminate the transformative power of stillness, demonstrating how it can enhance our connection to nature, foster intentional living, and facilitate a deeper understanding of ourselves.

Stillness serves as a gateway to cultivate presence in nature immersion. When we immerse ourselves in the natural world, quieting the mind and attuning our senses to the environment is essential. The sounds of rustling leaves, the gentle flow of water, and the subtle shifts of light beckon us to pause and engage fully.

By practicing stillness in these settings, we enhance our ability to observe and appreciate the intricate details of life that often go unnoticed. This heightened awareness enriches our outdoor experiences and deepens our gratitude for the natural world, reminding us of our interconnectedness with all living beings.

Intentional living, a philosophy that emphasizes aligning our actions with our core values, finds a powerful ally in stillness. When we carve out moments of quiet reflection, we understand what truly matters to us.

In the stillness, we can assess our choices and their alignment with our aspirations, making necessary adjustments to live authentically. This practice of self-reflection fosters a sense of purpose, guiding us toward decisions that resonate with our personal beliefs and desires. As we cultivate stillness in our lives, we develop a more profound understanding of ourselves, leading to a life that is not only intentional but also profoundly fulfilling.

The philosophy of non-action, particularly the principle of wuwei, encourages us to embrace stillness to navigate life's complexities. Wuwei teaches that the most effective way to approach challenges is often through relaxed awareness rather than forceful effort.

This perspective invites us to step back and allow situations to unfold naturally, which can lead to more organic and harmonious outcomes. By integrating the practice of stillness into our daily routines, we learn to approach life's difficulties with a sense of ease and calm, fostering resilience and adaptability in the face of adversity.

As we explore gratitude practices and the concept of amor fati, or love of fate, stillness becomes crucial in fostering acceptance. In moments of silence, we can reflect on our experiences, cultivating gratitude for both life's joyful and challenging aspects. This practice encourages us to embrace our circumstances fully, recognizing that every moment contributes to our growth and understanding.

Furthermore, disconnecting and embracing stillness can lead to a more meaningful existence in a digital age that often demands constant engagement. Sustainable living and a harmonious lifestyle emerge naturally when we prioritize stillness, allowing us to align our choices with the rhythms of nature and the deeper truths within ourselves.

The Cost of Constant Motion

Amid modern life's relentless pace, it's easy to lose sight of what truly matters. We're constantly bombarded by digital distractions, overscheduling, and overwhelm, leaving us fragmented and disconnected. Our minds are wired to respond instantly to notifications and distractions, fragmenting our attention spans and depleting our mental and emotional resources. As a result, we can no longer engage in deep contemplation or sustained focus, and our well-being suffers.

This culture that prioritizes productivity over presence leads to burnout, disconnection, and a host of mental health issues. We'll explore the impact of excessive stimulation, the rise of multitasking, and the erosion of mindfulness in modern life.

By examining the effects of a world that demands instant responses and constant activity, we'll see the value in reclaiming our lives and prioritizing presence over productivity.

As we delve into the challenges of modern life, we'll discover the importance of stillness in cultivating inner calm, self-awareness, and resilience.

We'll explore how embracing stillness can help us rebuild our fragmented attention spans, restore work-life balance, and deepen our connections with others and the natural world. By shedding light on the benefits of stillness, we'll begin to understand its profound impact on our mental, emotional, and physical well-being.

The Decline of Mindfulness in Modern Life

The relentless pace of modern life has eroded mindfulness, leaving us fragmented and disconnected. Constant digital distractions, overscheduling, and overwhelm have diminished our ability to be present as we struggle to maintain focus and concentration in a world that demands instant responses and constant multitasking.

This erosion of mindfulness has led to a culture of burnout, where the obsession with productivity and achievement has come at the expense of our well-being. We prioritize efficiency over presence, sacrificing our mental and emotional resources. As a result, we find ourselves depleted, disconnected, and overwhelmed by the constant barrage of sensory inputs from screens, media, and external demands.

The consequences of this are far-reaching. Our attention spans are fragmented, our minds racing from one stimulus to the next. We can no longer engage in deep contemplation or sustained focus, as our brains are wired to respond instantly to notifications and distractions. This overstimulation depletes our mental and emotional resources, leaving us vulnerable to stress, anxiety, and a range of other mental health issues.

In this chaotic landscape, losing sight of what truly matters is easy. We become trapped in a cycle of constant doing, rarely pausing, reflecting, and reconnecting with ourselves and the world around us. The absence of stillness and quiet contemplation has profound consequences for our mental, emotional, and physical well-being, leaving us feeling disconnected, drained, and on the brink of burnout.

It is time to reclaim our lives, prioritize presence over productivity, and rediscover the beauty of stillness. Doing so can rebuild our fragmented attention spans, calm our overwhelmed minds, and reconnect with the world. This is not a luxury but a necessity as we strive to find balance, harmony, and a more profound sense of meaning.

As we begin to prioritize stillness, we can start to see the world in a new light. We can appreciate the beauty of nature, the joy of quiet contemplation, and the peace that comes from being present in the moment. By embracing stillness, we can find the strength, clarity, and purpose we need to navigate the challenges of modern life with greater ease and confidence.

The Decline of Mindfulness in Modern Life

The relentless pace of modern life has eroded mindfulness, leaving us fragmented and disconnected. Constant digital distractions, overscheduling, and overwhelm have diminished our ability to be present as we struggle to maintain focus and concentration in a world that demands instant responses and constant multitasking.

This erosion of mindfulness has led to a culture of burnout, where the obsession with productivity and achievement has come at the expense of our well-being. We prioritize efficiency over presence, sacrificing our mental and emotional resources. As a result, we find ourselves depleted, disconnected, and overwhelmed by the constant barrage of sensory inputs from screens, media, and external demands.

The consequences of this are far-reaching. Our attention spans are fragmented, our minds racing from one stimulus to the next. We can no longer engage in deep contemplation or sustained focus, as our brains are wired to respond instantly to notifications and distractions. This overstimulation depletes our mental and emotional resources, leaving us vulnerable to stress, anxiety, and a range of other mental health issues.

In this chaotic landscape, losing sight of what truly matters is easy. We become trapped in a cycle of constant doing, rarely pausing, reflecting, and reconnecting with ourselves and the world around us. The absence of stillness and quiet contemplation has profound consequences for our mental, emotional, and physical well-being, leaving us feeling disconnected, drained, and on the brink of burnout.

It is time to reclaim our lives, prioritize presence over productivity, and rediscover the beauty of stillness. Doing so can rebuild our fragmented attention spans, calm our overwhelmed minds, and reconnect with the world. This is not a luxury but a necessity as we strive to find balance, harmony, and a more profound sense of meaning.

As we begin to prioritize stillness, we can start to see the world in a new light. We can appreciate the beauty of nature, the joy of quiet contemplation, and the peace that comes from being present in the moment. By embracing stillness, we can find the strength, clarity, and purpose we need to navigate the challenges of modern life with greater ease and confidence.

The Rise of Distraction and Its Consequences

.The constant influx of digital distractions has disrupted our ability to focus and be present. Smartphones, social media, and the always-on nature of technology have fractured our attention spans, making it challenging to engage deeply with tasks and experiences. This has severe consequences on our mental and physical health, with excessive screen time linked to eye strain, sleep disturbances, and increased anxiety.

The rise of multitasking has undermined our productivity and sense of accomplishment. By constantly switching between multiple devices and activities, we reduce our efficiency and the quality of our work, leaving us feeling overwhelmed and unfulfilled. This trend has become so prevalent that we often prioritize being constantly connected over being present at the moment.

Pursuing novelty and stimulation has reduced our appreciation for moments of stillness. The constant need for entertainment and new information has diminished our capacity to simply be, observe, and find joy in the present moment. As a result, we often sacrifice our well-being for the sake of instant gratification and distraction.

We must recognize the value of stillness to reclaim our time and attention. Incorporating moments of quiet contemplation into our daily routines allows us to develop a greater sense of awareness and presence. This, in turn, can lead to improved focus, reduced stress, and a deeper appreciation for life's simple pleasures.

It's not about cutting out technology entirely but finding a balance that allows us to engage meaningfully with the world. By being more intentional with our time and attention, we can create space for stillness and silence, leading to a more fulfilling and balanced life.

As we strive to navigate the complexities of modern life, it's crucial to acknowledge the importance of stillness. By prioritizing quiet contemplation and moments of silence, we can cultivate a greater sense of awareness, presence, and well-being. This, in turn, can lead to a more authentic and meaningful life that is less defined by constant distraction and more by a deep appreciation for the present moment.

The Importance of Non-Action

In a world that often equates productivity with worth, the concept of non-action emerges as a powerful antidote to the relentless pace of modern life. Non-action, or wuwei, invites individuals to embrace stillness and cultivate a deeper awareness of their surroundings and inner selves. This philosophy teaches that by stepping back and allowing life to unfold naturally, we can align ourselves more closely with our values and the natural world's rhythms. For those engaged in nature immersion and intentional living, understanding the importance of non-action can lead to profound transformations in how we experience and interact with our environment.

Non-action encourages a deep sense of presence, which is essential for those seeking to cultivate a meaningful connection with nature. Slowing down and observing the subtleties of the outdoors can help us gain a greater appreciation for the interconnectedness of all living things.

This immersion enhances our sensory experiences and allows us to reflect on our values and priorities. When we take the time to be simple, we open ourselves to insights that might otherwise be overlooked in the frenzy of daily life. Embracing non-action creates space for gratitude, enabling us to acknowledge the beauty and abundance surrounding us.

Incorporating the philosophy of non-action into our lives can also counterbalance the pressures of achievement and success. Many individuals in the modern world feel compelled to constantly strive for more, often at the expense of their well-being. By practicing non-action, we learn to let go of the need to control outcomes and instead trust in the natural flow of life.

This approach can lead to a more sustainable way of living, where our choices are guided by our core values rather than societal expectations. As we align our actions with our intentions, we create a fulfilling life that harmonizes with the broader ecological systems of which we are a part.

Digital detox is another area where the importance of non-action becomes evident. In our hyper-connected society, the constant barrage of information can create a sense of urgency that detracts from our ability to engage deeply with the present moment. By intentionally disconnecting from digital distractions, we allow ourselves the freedom to experience stillness and reflection.

This practice nurtures our capacity for gratitude as we become more attuned to life's simple pleasures. In this space of non-action, we can cultivate acceptance and embrace the philosophy of amor fati, learning to love our fate and circumstances, irrespective of their challenges.

Ultimately, the importance of non-action lies in its potential to foster a profound sense of balance in our lives. As we navigate the intersection of Eastern philosophy and Western wellness practices, we discover that stillness is not merely the absence of activity but a deliberate choice that enriches our existence.

We cultivate resilience, clarity, and a deeper connection to ourselves and the natural world by embracing non-action. This journey toward balance encourages us to rethink our relationship with time, productivity, and fulfillment, inviting us to step into a life that honors our individuality and place within the larger tapestry of existence.

The Necessity of Balance in a Fast-Paced World

Maintaining a healthy equilibrium between activity and calm is crucial for well-being. The frenetic pace of modern life demands a counterbalance of stillness, and embracing stillness allows for deeper focus, creativity, and meaningful connection. Moments of quiet reflection and non-action recharge the mind and spirit while incorporating pauses and moments of tranquility mitigates the adverse effects of over-activity.

Constant stimulation and distractions can lead to burnout, anxiety, and disconnection. Integrating stillness practices into daily routines promotes greater work-life harmony, and seeking balance through stillness cultivates a more intentional and fulfilling lifestyle. The power of stillness lies in its ability to ground us in the present, enhancing our awareness and appreciation of life.

When prioritizing stillness, we create space for our minds and bodies to rest and recharge. This, in turn, allows us to approach challenges with a more precise and focused mind, leading to improved decision-making and problem-solving skills. Stillness also enables us to cultivate more profound self-awareness, which is essential for making intentional choices and living more authentically.

Incorporating stillness into our daily lives can be as simple as taking a few deep breaths before a meeting, practicing yoga or meditation, or simply walking in nature. By prioritizing stillness, we can reduce stress and anxiety, improve our mood, and increase our overall well-being.

Furthermore, stillness has a profound impact on our creativity and productivity. When we reflect and recharge, we allow ourselves to tap into our creative potential and approach problems with a fresh perspective. This, in turn, can lead to innovative solutions and new ideas.
In a world that values productivity and activity above all else, stillness is often seen as a luxury or a chore.

However, we must recognize the value of stillness and prioritize it in our lives. Doing so can improve our mental and physical health, increase our creativity and productivity, and help us live more intentionally and fulfillingly.

We can create a more harmonious and peaceful existence by embracing stillness and prioritizing balance in our lives. We can learn to appreciate the beauty of quiet moments and find peace and calm amid chaos. By prioritizing stillness, we can live more intentionally and approach life with greater clarity and purpose.

In today's fast-paced world, it's easy to get caught up in the hustle and bustle of daily life. However, we can create a more balanced and fulfilling life by incorporating stillness into our daily routines. We can learn to appreciate the beauty of quiet moments and find peace and calm amid chaos. By prioritizing stillness, we can live more intentionally and approach life with greater clarity and purpose.
Finding a balance between activity and stillness is a personal and ongoing process. It requires intention, commitment, and self-awareness. We can cultivate a greater sense of calm, clarity, and

purpose by prioritizing stillness and making it a regular part of our lives. We can live more intentionally, make more mindful choices, and approach life's challenges more quickly and confidently.

The Necessity of Balance in a Fast-Paced World

Maintaining a healthy equilibrium between activity and calm is crucial for well-being. The frenetic pace of modern life demands a counterbalance of stillness, and embracing stillness allows for deeper focus, creativity, and meaningful connection. Moments of quiet reflection and non-action recharge the mind and spirit while incorporating pauses and moments of tranquility mitigates the harmful effects of over-activity.

Constant stimulation and distractions can lead to burnout, anxiety, and disconnection. Integrating stillness practices into daily routines promotes greater work-life harmony, and seeking balance through stillness cultivates a more intentional and fulfilling lifestyle. The power of stillness lies in its ability to ground us in the present, enhancing our awareness and appreciation of life.

When prioritizing stillness, we create space for our minds and bodies to rest and recharge. This, in turn, allows us to approach challenges with a more precise and focused mind, leading to improved decision-making and problem-solving skills. Stillness also enables us to cultivate more profound self-awareness, which is essential for making intentional choices and living more authentically.

Incorporating stillness into our daily lives can be as simple as taking a few deep breaths before a meeting, practicing yoga or meditation, or simply walking in nature. By prioritizing stillness, we can reduce stress and anxiety, improve our mood, and increase our overall well-being.

Furthermore, stillness has a profound impact on our creativity and productivity. When we reflect and recharge, we allow ourselves to tap into our creative potential and approach problems with a fresh perspective. This, in turn, can lead to innovative solutions and new ideas.

In a world that values productivity and activity above all else, stillness is often seen as a luxury or a chore. However, we must recognize the value of stillness and prioritize it in our lives. Doing so can improve our mental and physical health, increase our creativity and productivity, and live more intentional and fulfilling lives.

By embracing stillness and prioritizing balance, we can create a more harmonious and peaceful existence. We can learn to appreciate the beauty of quiet moments and find peace and calm amid chaos. By prioritizing stillness, we can live more intentionally and approach life with greater clarity and purpose.

In today's fast-paced world, it's easy to get caught up in the hustle and bustle of daily life. However, we can create a more balanced and fulfilling life by incorporating stillness into our daily routines. We can learn to appreciate the beauty of quiet moments and find peace and calm amid chaos. By prioritizing stillness, we can live more intentionally and approach life with greater clarity and purpose.

Finding a balance between activity and stillness is a personal and ongoing process. It requires intention, commitment, and self-awareness. We can cultivate a greater sense of calm, clarity, and purpose by prioritizing stillness and making it a regular part of our lives. We can live more intentionally, make more mindful choices, and approach life's challenges more quickly and confidently.

The transformative power of stillness

The transformative power of stillness lies in its remarkable ability to forge a deep and meaningful connection between the mind, body, and spirit. In today's fast-paced world, characterized by constant noise, distractions, and relentless activity, finding moments to embrace stillness becomes beneficial and essential.

These precious pauses provide a necessary refuge, inviting us to retreat from the chaos and take a reflective breath. Within this sanctuary of calm, we can reconnect with our inner selves, allowing clarity and awareness to emerge—qualities frequently drowned out by everyday life's constant demands and distractions.

When we consciously grant ourselves the opportunity to be still, we cultivate a heightened sense of mindfulness. This practice encourages us to delve deeper into our thoughts, emotions, and desires, fostering a more profound self-awareness. With this increased awareness, we become empowered to make intentional choices that resonate with our core values and aspirations. Our actions align more authentically with who we are, transforming our lives into a more deliberate journey.

Furthermore, stillness is pivotal in building resilience, particularly during stress, upheaval, or uncertainty. Deliberately immersing ourselves in stillness can be a powerful strategy for regaining our composure and shifting our perspective.

Grounding ourselves amidst chaos helps us embrace life's natural ebb and flow, fostering an understanding that challenges and obstacles are inherent in the human experience. By cultivating this acceptance, we can develop more outstanding emotional balance, equipping ourselves with the tools to navigate the tumultuous waves of uncertainty with grace, courage, and resilience.

Ultimately, incorporating stillness into our daily lives can transform us and guide us toward greater authenticity, inner peace, and fulfillment.

This journey invites us not just to exist but to thrive, nurturing our overall well-being and enabling us to respond to life's challenges with an open heart and a clear mind. By recognizing the profound benefits of stillness, we can learn to cherish these moments of quiet reflection as essential components of a balanced and enriched life.

The Historical Significance of Stillness in Human Experience

The concept of stillness has been a cornerstone of human experience throughout history, with diverse cultures and spiritual traditions emphasizing its transformative power. Ancient Eastern philosophies, such as Taoism and Buddhism, have long recognized the value of stillness, non-action, and the cultivation of presence as essential to personal growth and enlightenment. In these traditions, stillness connects with the natural world and the deeper aspects of one's being.

Similarly, Western religious and philosophical traditions, from monastic contemplation to Stoic meditation, have recognized the transformative power of stillness and its ability to foster self-awareness and inner peace. Historically, periods of silence and solitude have allowed humans to reconnect with nature, the sacred, and the deeper aspects of their being, providing a respite from the demands of daily life.

Throughout history, artists, writers, and thinkers have sought to capture the essence of stillness, using it as a source of inspiration and a means of conveying the depth of human experience. From the serene landscapes of Claude Monet to the meditative poems of Rainer Maria Rilke, stillness has been a recurring theme in the creative works of many notable figures.

In an increasingly fast-paced and technology-driven world, the historical significance of stillness has become even more relevant. As individuals and societies grapple with the need to find balance and reconnect with the present moment, the concept of stillness offers a valuable framework for understanding and achieving this goal.

Cultivating stillness can help individuals develop self-awareness, clarity, and purpose, leading to a more authentic and fulfilling life.

The concept of stillness, as described by Carl Jung, has also been recognized as a means of tapping into the collective unconscious. According to Jung, stillness allows individuals to access the deeper aspects of their psyche, where the unconscious mind resides. This access can lead to greater insight, creativity, and personal growth.

The importance of stillness cannot be overstated in an increasingly fast-paced world. Stillness offers a valuable means of reconnecting with the present moment and finding balance in a chaotic world.

By embracing stillness, individuals can cultivate a deeper understanding of themselves and the world around them, leading to a more authentic and fulfilling life.

The power of stillness lies in its ability to help us quiet the mind, focus on the present moment, and connect with our deeper selves. By embracing stillness, we can tap into our creativity, access our unconscious mind, and develop greater self-awareness.

In today's world, where constant distractions and pressures can leave us feeling overwhelmed and disconnected, the concept of stillness offers a powerful antidote.

Ultimately, the concept of stillness is not just a philosophical idea but a practical tool for achieving balance, self-awareness, and inner peace. By embracing stillness, we can cultivate a deeper understanding of ourselves and the world around us, leading to a more authentic and meaningful life. As we move forward in our quest for personal growth and self-awareness, the concept of stillness will continue to play a vital role in our journey.

The concept of stillness has been a cornerstone of human experience throughout history, with diverse cultures and spiritual traditions emphasizing its transformative power. By recognizing the value of stillness and incorporating it into our daily lives, we can develop a greater sense of clarity, purpose, and fulfillment, leading to a more authentic and meaningful existence.

In today's world, where constant distractions and pressures can leave us feeling overwhelmed and disconnected, stillness offers a valuable means of achieving balance, self-awareness, and inner peace. By embracing stillness, individuals can develop greater self-awareness, clarity, and purpose, leading to a more authentic and fulfilling life.

The concept of stillness has been a cornerstone of human experience throughout history, with diverse cultures and spiritual traditions emphasizing its transformative power. As we navigate the challenges of modern life, stillness offers a valuable framework for achieving balance, self-awareness, and inner peace. By embracing stillness, we can cultivate a deeper understanding of ourselves and the world around us, leading to a more authentic and meaningful existence.

The concept of stillness is a means of connecting with the natural world and the deeper aspects of one's being. Cultivating stillness can lead to greater self-awareness, clarity, and purpose, leading to a more authentic and fulfilling life. In an increasingly fast-paced world, the importance of stillness cannot be overstated. It offers a valuable means of reconnecting with the present moment and finding balance in a chaotic world.

In today's world, stillness offers a powerful antidote to the constant distractions and pressures that can leave us feeling overwhelmed and disconnected.

By embracing stillness, individuals can tap into their creativity, access their unconscious mind, and develop a greater self-awareness, leading to a more authentic and fulfilling life.
The concept of stillness is a practical tool for achieving balance, self-awareness, and inner peace.

By embracing stillness, we can cultivate a deeper understanding of ourselves and the world around us, leading to a more authentic and meaningful existence. As we move forward in our quest for personal growth and self-awareness, the concept of stillness will continue to play a vital role in our journey.

The concept of stillness has been a cornerstone of human experience throughout history, with diverse cultures and spiritual traditions emphasizing its transformative power. By recognizing the value of stillness and incorporating it into our daily lives, we can develop a greater sense of clarity, purpose, and fulfillment, leading to a more authentic and meaningful existence.

In an increasingly fast-paced world, the importance of stillness cannot be overstated. Stillness offers a valuable means of reconnecting with the present moment and finding balance in a chaotic world. By embracing stillness, individuals can cultivate a deeper understanding of themselves and the world around them, leading to a more authentic and fulfilling life.

The concept of stillness is a means of tapping into the collective unconscious. It allows individuals to access the deeper aspects of their psyche and develop a greater sense of self-awareness. By embracing stillness, we can quiet the mind, focus on the present moment, and connect with our deeper selves, leading to a more authentic and fulfilling life.

The concept of stillness has been a cornerstone of human experience throughout history, with diverse cultures and spiritual traditions emphasizing its transformative power. By recognizing the value of stillness and incorporating it into our daily lives, we can develop a greater sense of clarity, purpose, and fulfillment, leading to a more authentic and meaningful existence.

The concept of stillness is a means of achieving balance, self-awareness, and inner peace in a chaotic world. By embracing stillness, individuals can cultivate a deeper understanding of themselves and the world around them, leading to a more authentic and fulfilling life. In today's world, the concept of stillness offers a powerful antidote to the constant distractions and pressures that can leave us feeling overwhelmed and disconnected.

The concept of stillness has been a cornerstone of human experience throughout history, with diverse cultures and spiritual traditions emphasizing its transformative power. As we navigate the challenges of modern life, stillness offers a valuable framework for achieving balance, self-awareness, and inner peace. By embracing stillness, we can cultivate a deeper understanding of ourselves and the world around us, leading to a more authentic and meaningful existence.

The concept of stillness has been a cornerstone of human experience throughout history, with diverse cultures and spiritual traditions emphasizing its transformative power. By recognizing the value of stillness and incorporating it into our daily lives, we can develop a greater sense of clarity, purpose, and fulfillment, leading to a more authentic and meaningful existence.

In an increasingly fast-paced world, the importance of stillness cannot be overstated. Stillness offers a valuable means of reconnecting with the present moment and finding balance in a chaotic world. By embracing stillness, individuals can cultivate a deeper understanding of themselves and the world around them, leading to a more authentic and fulfilling life.

The concept of stillness is a means of tapping into the collective unconscious, allowing individuals to access the deeper aspects of their psyche and develop a greater sense of self-awareness. By embracing stillness, we can quiet the mind, focus on the present moment, and connect with our deeper selves, leading to a more authentic and fulfilling life.

The Promise of Stillness in a Chaotic World

In today's fast-paced world, the promise of stillness offers a much-needed respite from the relentless pace and overwhelming demands of modern life. Stillness provides peace and clarity, allowing individuals to recharge and refocus. By embracing stillness, individuals can develop greater self-awareness, emotional regulation, and resilience in the face of external turmoil.

One key benefit of stillness is its ability to restore work-life balance. By incorporating moments of stillness into one's daily routine, individuals can combat burnout and enhance overall productivity and well-being. This can be achieved through simple practices such as meditation, deep breathing, or spending time in nature. By slowing down and being present, individuals can also deepen their connections with others, fostering a greater sense of community and belonging.

In addition to its benefits, stillness can profoundly impact our relationship with the natural world. Immersing oneself in the stillness of the environment can foster a deeper appreciation for the rhythms of nature and one's place within it. This can be achieved through hiking, gardening, or simply outdoors. By reconnecting with nature, individuals can gain a new perspective on life and develop a greater sense of wonder and awe.

Stillness can also unlock creative potential by quieting the mind and allowing for greater focus and clarity. This can be especially beneficial for individuals in creative fields, such as artists, writers, or musicians. Individuals can tap into their inner voice and aspirations by cultivating stillness, leading to greater innovation and productivity.

In a world that increasingly values busyness and productivity, the promise of stillness is a powerful reminder of the importance of slowing down and being present. By embracing stillness, individuals can develop self-awareness, emotional regulation, and resilience, leading to a more balanced and fulfilling life. Whether through meditation, nature, or creative pursuits, stillness offers a powerful tool for personal growth and transformation.

As we navigate the challenges of modern life, stillness offers a powerful reminder of the importance of balance and harmony. Cultivating stillness can help individuals develop self-awareness, emotional regulation, and resilience, leading to a more balanced and fulfilling life. Stillness is a powerful tool for personal growth and transformation, essential to a healthy and balanced lifestyle.

In a world that increasingly values productivity and efficiency, the promise of stillness is a powerful reminder of the importance of slowing down and being present. By embracing stillness, individuals can develop self-awareness, emotional regulation, and resilience, leading to a more balanced and fulfilling life. As we move forward in an increasingly fast-paced world, the promise of stillness offers a powerful reminder of the importance of balance and harmony.
The promise of stillness is a powerful reminder of the importance of balance and harmony in our lives.

By embracing stillness, individuals can develop self-awareness, emotional regulation, and resilience, leading to a more balanced and fulfilling life. Whether through simple practices such as meditation or deep breathing or more immersive experiences such as nature or creative pursuits, stillness offers a powerful tool for personal growth and transformation.

Stillness offers a powerful tool for personal growth and transformation. By embracing stillness, individuals can develop self-awareness, emotional regulation, and resilience, leading to a more balanced and fulfilling life. Whether through simple practices such as meditation or deep breathing or more immersive experiences such as nature or creative pursuits, stillness is a powerful reminder of the importance of balance and harmony.

In a world that increasingly values productivity and efficiency, the promise of stillness is a powerful reminder of the importance of slowing down and being present.

By embracing stillness, individuals can develop self-awareness, emotional regulation, and resilience, leading to a more balanced and fulfilling life. As we move forward in an increasingly fast-paced world, the promise of stillness offers a powerful reminder of the importance of balance and harmony.

Stillness can profoundly impact our relationships with others. By slowing down and being present, individuals can deepen their connections with others, fostering a greater sense of community and belonging. This can be especially beneficial in today's world, where many people feel disconnected and isolated.

The promise of stillness is a powerful reminder of the importance of caring for ourselves. By embracing stillness, individuals can develop self-awareness, emotional regulation, and resilience, leading to a more balanced and fulfilling life.

Whether through simple practices such as meditation or deep breathing or more immersive experiences such as nature or creative pursuits, stillness offers a powerful tool for personal growth and transformation.

As we navigate the challenges of modern life, stillness offers a powerful reminder of the importance of balance and harmony. Cultivating stillness can help individuals develop self-awareness, emotional regulation, and resilience, leading to a more balanced and fulfilling life. Stillness is a powerful tool for personal growth and transformation essential to a healthy and balanced lifestyle.

In a world that increasingly values productivity and efficiency, the promise of stillness is a powerful reminder of the importance of slowing down and being present. By embracing stillness, individuals can develop self-awareness, emotional regulation, and resilience, leading to a more balanced and fulfilling life.

As we move forward in an increasingly fast-paced world, the promise of stillness offers a powerful reminder of the importance of balance and harmony.

Stillness powerfully reminds us of the importance of taking care of ourselves. By embracing stillness, individuals can develop self-awareness, emotional regulation, and resilience, leading to a more balanced and fulfilling life.

Whether through simple practices such as meditation or deep breathing or more immersive experiences such as nature or creative pursuits, stillness offers a powerful tool for personal growth and transformation.

As we move forward in an increasingly fast-paced world, the promise of stillness offers a powerful reminder of the importance of balance and harmony. By embracing stillness, individuals can develop self-awareness, emotional regulation, and resilience, leading to a more balanced and fulfilling life. Stillness offers a powerful tool for personal growth and transformation, an essential component of a healthy and balanced lifestyle.

In a world that increasingly values productivity and efficiency, the promise of stillness is a powerful reminder of the importance of slowing down and being present.

By embracing stillness, individuals can develop self-awareness, emotional regulation, and resilience, leading to a more balanced and fulfilling life. As we navigate the challenges of modern life, stillness offers a powerful reminder of the importance of balance and harmony.

Exploring the Concept of Stillness

Amid life's chaos, we often struggle to find calm and clarity. The mind is a whirlwind of thoughts, emotions, and distractions, challenging to access inner peace and awareness. Yet within us lies a profound capacity for stillness, a state that is not just a passive absence of noise but a vibrant, living presence that can transform our lives.

Recognizing the interconnectedness of our being – the intricate web of mind, body, and spirit – is the first step toward cultivating true stillness. By acknowledging the ripple effects of imbalance and nurturing the connections between our inner selves, we can quiet the mind, soothe the body, and stimulate the spirit.

As we delve into the practice of stillness, we will explore the essential connection between mental calm, physical balance, and spiritual nourishment. We will examine how stillness can be cultivated through mindfulness, breathwork, and movement and how it can infuse our lives with meaning and transcendence. We will also explore the rich heritage of spiritual traditions that have long recognized the value of stillness in achieving inner peace, self-awareness, and a deeper connection with the world around us.

Through the lens of stillness, we will discover the profound benefits of this practice, from reduced stress and improved physical health to enhanced focus, creativity, and a more profound sense of purpose. We will learn how to harness the power of stillness to navigate life's challenges with greater resilience and presence and integrate it into our daily lives to cultivate a sense of inner peace and external harmony.

In the following pages, we will explore the practical aspects of cultivating stillness, from mindfulness and breathwork to movement and sensory immersion. We will examine the scientific benefits of stillness, from reduced cortisol levels to improved brain function, and we will delve into the rich spiritual traditions that have long recognized the value of stillness in achieving inner peace and self-awareness.

Our goal is not to add another practice to our already crowded lives but to integrate stillness into our being, allowing us to live with greater clarity, purpose, and joy.

The Interconnectedness of Mind, Body, and Spirit

Recognizing the interconnectedness of our being is the foundation for cultivating true stillness. The mind, body, and spirit are intricately linked, and understanding this relationship is key to achieving balance and harmony. When one aspect of our being is out of alignment, it can ripple effect on the others, leading to feelings of disquiet and unrest. By acknowledging and addressing these connections, we can quiet the mind, soothe the body, and nurture the spirit.

This, in turn, allows us to tap into a sense of inner peace and calm, even amid chaos. Regular practice makes it easier to quiet the mind and connect with our thoughts and emotions more authentically. This, in turn, can lead to a greater sense of calm and clarity, enabling us to make more intentional decisions and live more intentionally. By recognizing the holistic nature of our being, we can begin to make choices that support our well-being and foster a more profound sense of stillness.

Mental calm and clarity allow us to access a state of inner peace and awareness. This state is characterized by a quiet mind, free from distractions and chatter. Regular mindfulness and meditation practice can help calm the mind and increase self-awareness.

By cultivating mental calm and clarity, we can easily navigate life's challenges and find a more profound inner peace. Regular practice makes it easier to quiet the mind and connect with our thoughts and emotions more authentically.

This, in turn, can lead to a greater sense of calm and clarity, enabling us to make more intentional decisions and live more intentionally. A calm and clear mind is essential for a more fulfilling and meaningful life. Furthermore, the physical body and mind are intricately connected, and practices like meditation, breathwork, and mindful movement can bring the body into balance and relaxation, further enhancing this sense of inner calm and clarity.

The physical body and mind are intricately connected, and practices like meditation, breathwork, and mindful movement bring the body into balance and relaxation. By focusing on the present moment, individuals can quiet the mind and release physical tension, decreasing stress, improving sleep, and experiencing greater well-being.

This balance between body and mind can promote physical health, including reduced blood pressure and a more muscular immune system. As we cultivate this connection, we become more grounded and at peace, finding meaning and fulfillment in our lives.

Nourishing the spiritual dimension requires a deep connection to the natural world, which infuses our lives with a sense of belonging, purpose, and transcendence. By embracing stillness, we can tap into our inner selves and align with the world around us, guided by our passions and values toward a life of intention and direction.

Nourishing the spiritual dimension requires a deep connection to the natural world. This connection infuses our lives with meaning and transcendence. By embracing stillness, we can tap into our inner selves and align with the world. In nature, we find a sense of belonging and unity with the universe.

Our purpose is revealed through our passions and values, guiding us towards a life of intention and direction. A sense of the divine reminds us of our place and inspires us to live with compassion and kindness. As we cultivate this connection, we become more grounded and at peace, finding meaning and fulfillment in our lives.

The Role of Stillness in Spiritual and Philosophical Traditions

Stillness is a central concept in various spiritual and philosophical schools of thought, serving as a foundation for inner peace, contemplation, and self-discovery. Eastern philosophies, such as Taoism and Buddhism, emphasize the importance of stillness, or "wu wei," to align with the natural flow of the universe and achieve a state of effortless action. This principle is often associated with harmony with the natural world and allowing things to unfold without forced intervention.

In contrast, Western philosophical traditions, including Stoicism and mindfulness-based practices, recognize the value of stillness in cultivating self-awareness, emotional regulation, and a deeper understanding of one's place in the world. Stoicism, for instance, teaches individuals to observe their thoughts and emotions without judgment, allowing them to respond to challenging situations with greater wisdom and serenity.

Many spiritual traditions, such as Hinduism and Sufism, view stillness as a means to achieve higher states of consciousness, spiritual awakening, and a deeper connection with the divine or the true self. These traditions often emphasize the importance of quiet contemplation, meditation, and prayer to cultivate inner stillness and connect with a higher reality.

The benefits of stillness are numerous and far-reaching. By embracing stillness, individuals can experience a greater sense of inner calm, clarity, and the ability to navigate life's challenges with greater resilience and presence.

Stillness can also help individuals develop greater self-awareness, allowing them better to understand their values, goals, and motivations.

In a world dominated by constant movement and distraction, stillness offers a much-needed respite from the demands of modern life. We can cultivate a greater sense of balance, harmony, and well-being by incorporating stillness into our daily routines. This, in turn, can lead to more intentional living, deeper relationships, and a greater sense of purpose and fulfillment.

Incorporating stillness into our lives can be as simple as taking a few moments to breathe deeply, practicing mindfulness, or engaging in quiet contemplation. By making stillness a regular part of our lives, we can experience a more profound connection to ourselves, others, and the world around us. Stillness offers a powerful path to inner peace, self-discovery, and a more meaningful life.

The concept of stillness is not just a theory; it is a practice that can be cultivated through mindfulness, meditation, and other forms of quiet contemplation. By making stillness a regular part of our lives, we can experience more excellent balance, harmony, and well-being, leading to more intentional living, deeper relationships, and a greater sense of purpose and fulfillment.

Stillness is a luxury and a necessity for living a balanced, harmonious, and meaningful life. By embracing stillness, individuals can experience more excellent balance, harmony, and well-being, leading to more intentional living, deeper relationships, and a greater sense of purpose and fulfillment. Stillness offers a powerful tool for cultivating inner peace, self-discovery, and a more meaningful life.

By incorporating stillness into our lives, we can experience a greater sense of connection to ourselves, others, and the world around us. Stillness offers a powerful path to inner peace, self-discovery, and a more meaningful life, making it an essential component of any spiritual or personal growth practice.

Stillness is vital to many spiritual and philosophical traditions, offering a powerful path to inner peace, self-discovery, and a more meaningful life. By embracing stillness, individuals can cultivate a greater sense of balance, harmony, and well-being, leading to more intentional living, deeper relationships, and a greater understanding of purpose and fulfillment.

Stillness offers a powerful tool for cultivating inner peace, self-discovery, and a more meaningful life. We can develop a greater sense of balance, harmony, and well-being by incorporating stillness into our daily routines. This, in turn, can lead to more intentional living, deeper relationships, and a greater sense of purpose and fulfillment.

The benefits of stillness are numerous and far-reaching. By embracing stillness, individuals can experience a greater sense of inner calm and clarity and the ability to navigate life's challenges with greater resilience and presence. Stillness can also help individuals develop greater self-awareness, allowing them to better understand their values, goals, and motivations.

Stillness offers a much-needed counterbalance in a world that increasingly values action and productivity. By embracing stillness, individuals can experience more excellent balance, harmony, and well-being, leading to more intentional living, deeper relationships, and a greater sense of purpose and fulfillment.

By incorporating stillness into our lives, we can experience a more profound connection to ourselves, others, and the world around us. Stillness offers a powerful path to inner peace, self-discovery, and a more meaningful life, making it an essential component of any spiritual or personal growth practice.

Stillness is not just a concept; it is a practice that can be cultivated through mindfulness, meditation, and other forms of quiet contemplation. By making stillness a regular part of our lives, we can experience more excellent balance, harmony, and well-being, leading to more intentional living, deeper relationships, and a greater sense of purpose and fulfillment.

The Science Behind the Benefits of Stillness

Stillness has been widely recognized for its profound impact on physical and mental well-being. One of its most significant benefits is its ability to activate the parasympathetic nervous system, which reduces stress and promotes relaxation.

This, in turn, can positively affect overall physical health, as a regular practice of stillness has been shown to lower blood pressure, heart rate, and cortisol levels.

In addition to its physical benefits, stillness has profoundly impacted emotional regulation. By reducing activity in the amygdala, the part of the brain responsible for processing fear and anxiety, stillness can help to calm the mind and promote a sense of emotional balance. This can be particularly beneficial for individuals who struggle with anxiety or other emotional challenges.

Stillness has also positively impacted cognitive function, mainly focus, memory, and information processing. By increasing brain activity in the prefrontal cortex, stillness can help to improve attention and concentration, making it easier to learn and remember new information. This can be particularly beneficial for individuals looking to enhance their cognitive abilities.

One of the most significant benefits of stillness is its ability to cultivate self-awareness, which is the ability to observe one's thoughts, emotions, and behaviors with clarity and precision.

By developing self-awareness, individuals can better understand themselves and their place in the world, creating a greater sense of meaning and purpose. This can be particularly beneficial for individuals who want to better understand the direction and purpose of their lives.

In today's fast-paced world, it can be easy to get caught up in the hustle and bustle of daily life and lose sight of what is truly important. Stillness offers a powerful antidote, allowing individuals to slow down, reflect, and connect with their inner selves.

Incorporating stillness into our daily lives can cultivate a greater sense of balance, harmony, and well-being, leading to a more fulfilling and intentional life.

Incorporating stillness into our daily lives can be as simple as taking a few minutes each day to sit quietly, practice deep breathing, or engage in a relaxing activity such as reading or listening to music. It can also involve incorporating physical activities such as yoga or tai chi, which can help to cultivate a sense of stillness and balance in the body.

By making stillness a regular part of our lives, we can experience various benefits, from reduced stress and anxiety to improved cognitive function and greater self-awareness.

Stillness is a powerful tool for cultivating balance, harmony, and well-being. By incorporating stillness into our daily lives, we can experience various benefits leading to a more fulfilling and intentional life. Through meditation, deep breathing, or physical activity, stillness allows individuals to slow down, reflect, and connect with their inner selves.

By making stillness a regular part of our lives, we can cultivate a greater sense of balance, harmony, and well-being, leading to a more fulfilling and intentional life. This can be achieved by taking a few minutes daily to sit quietly, practice deep breathing, or engage in a relaxing activity. It is a simple yet powerful tool that can profoundly impact physical and mental well-being.

Regular practice of stillness can significantly impact our overall quality of life. It can help reduce stress and anxiety, improve cognitive function, and cultivate greater self-awareness. By incorporating stillness into our daily lives, we can experience various benefits leading to a more fulfilling and intentional life.

Individuals can better understand themselves and their place in the world by developing self-awareness. This can lead to a greater sense of meaning, purpose, direction, and purpose in life. Stillness offers a powerful tool for cultivating self-awareness, and by making it a regular part of our lives, we can experience a range of benefits that can lead to a more fulfilling and intentional life.

Stillness is a simple yet powerful tool that can profoundly impact physical and mental well-being. By incorporating stillness into our daily lives, we can experience various benefits leading to a more fulfilling and intentional life. Through meditation, deep breathing, or physical activity, stillness allows individuals to slow down, reflect, and connect with their inner selves.

Incorporating stillness into our daily lives can be a transformative experience. It allows us to tap into our inner wisdom and better understand ourselves and our world. By making stillness a regular part of our lives, we can cultivate a greater sense of balance, harmony, and well-being, leading to a more fulfilling and intentional life.

Regular practice of stillness can lead to a range of benefits, from reduced stress and anxiety to improved cognitive function and a greater sense of self-awareness. By making stillness a regular part of our lives, we can experience a more fulfilling and intentional life characterized by balance, harmony, and well-being.

In today's fast-paced world, it can be easy to get caught up in the hustle and bustle of daily life and lose sight of what is truly important. Stillness offers a powerful antidote, allowing individuals to slow down, reflect, and connect with their inner selves. Incorporating stillness into our daily lives can cultivate a greater sense of balance, harmony, and well-being, leading to a more fulfilling and intentional life.

Stillness is a simple yet powerful tool that can profoundly impact physical and mental well-being. By incorporating stillness into our daily lives, we can experience various benefits leading to a more fulfilling and intentional life. Through meditation, deep breathing, or physical activity, stillness allows individuals to slow down, reflect, and connect with their inner selves.

By making stillness a regular part of our lives, we can cultivate a greater sense of balance, harmony, and well-being, leading to a more fulfilling and intentional life. This can be achieved by taking a few minutes daily to sit quietly, practice deep breathing, or engage in a relaxing activity. It is a simple yet powerful tool that can profoundly impact physical and mental well-being.

Regular practice of stillness can significantly impact our overall quality of life. It can help reduce stress and anxiety, improve cognitive function, and cultivate greater self-awareness. By incorporating stillness into our daily lives, we can experience various benefits leading to a more fulfilling and intentional life.

Individuals can better understand themselves and their place in the world by developing self-awareness. This can lead to a greater sense of meaning, purpose, direction, and purpose in life. Stillness offers a powerful tool for cultivating self-awareness, and by making it a regular part of our lives, we can experience a range of benefits that can lead to a more fulfilling and intentional life.

Incorporating stillness into our daily lives can cultivate a greater sense of balance, harmony, and well-being, leading to a more fulfilling and intentional life. This can be achieved by taking a few minutes daily to sit quietly, practice deep breathing, or engage in a relaxing activity. It is a simple yet powerful tool that can profoundly impact physical and mental well-being.

Regular practice of stillness can lead to a range of benefits, from reduced stress and anxiety to improved cognitive function and a greater sense of self-awareness. By making stillness a regular part of our lives, we can experience a more fulfilling and intentional life characterized by balance, harmony, and well-being.

Stillness is a powerful tool for cultivating balance, harmony, and well-being. By incorporating stillness into our daily lives, we can experience various benefits leading to a more fulfilling and intentional life. Through meditation, deep breathing, or physical activity, stillness allows individuals to slow down, reflect, and connect with their inner selves.

By making stillness a regular part of our lives, we can cultivate a greater sense of balance, harmony, and well-being, leading to a more fulfilling and intentional life. This can be achieved by taking a few minutes daily to sit quietly, practice deep breathing, or engage in a relaxing activity. It is a simple yet powerful tool that can profoundly impact physical and mental well-being.

In today's fast-paced world, it can be easy to get caught up in the hustle and bustle of daily life and lose sight of what is truly important. Stillness offers a powerful antidote, allowing individuals to slow down, reflect, and connect with their inner selves. Incorporating stillness into our daily lives can cultivate a greater sense of balance, harmony, and well-being, leading to a more fulfilling and intentional life.

Stillness is a simple yet powerful tool that can profoundly impact physical and mental well-being. By incorporating stillness into our daily lives, we can experience various benefits leading to a more fulfilling and intentional life.

Through meditation, deep breathing, or physical activity, stillness allows individuals to slow down, reflect, and connect with their inner selves.

Incorporating stillness into our daily lives can be a transformative experience. It allows us to tap into our inner wisdom and better understand ourselves and our world. By making stillness a regular part of our lives, we can cultivate a greater sense of balance, harmony, and well-being, leading to a more fulfilling and intentional life.

Regular practice of stillness can lead to a range of benefits, from reduced stress and anxiety to improved cognitive function and a greater sense of self-awareness. By making stillness a regular part of our lives, we can experience a more fulfilling and intentional life characterized by balance, harmony, and well-being.

The Intersection of Stillness and Intentionality

The intersection of stillness and intentionality is a crucial foundation for a balanced life. It allows us to pause, reflect, and become more aware of our thoughts, emotions, and actions. This heightened self-awareness enables us to make more conscious and purposeful decisions in our daily lives, aligning our actions with our deeper purpose and desires.

Integrating stillness and intentionality can help us experience inner peace and external harmony. We become more mindful, present, and connected to the world around us. This balance allows us to quickly cultivate meaningful relationships, navigate life's challenges, and find fulfillment in our pursuits.

When we cultivate stillness, we gain the clarity and focus to make intentional choices that align with our values and priorities. We move away from reactivity towards proactive, meaningful engagement with the world. This shift in perspective enables us to respond to situations rather than react to them, leading to more effective and fulfilling interactions.

Stillness also allows us to become more aware of our emotions and thoughts, enabling us to make more informed decisions. Acknowledging and accepting our feelings, we can respond to challenging situations with greater ease and composure. This increased self-awareness helps us recognize and challenge negative thought patterns, leading to a more positive and empowered mindset.

The balance between stillness and intentionality is essential for sustainable personal growth and self-actualization. Cultivating this balance can help us experience a sense of purpose and direction. We can become more aware of our strengths and weaknesses and use this knowledge to make intentional choices that support our growth and well-being.

Incorporating stillness and intentionality into our daily lives can be as simple as taking a few minutes each day to practice deep breathing or engage in a creative activity. By prioritizing these practices, we can experience the many benefits of stillness and intentionality, including increased self-awareness, improved decision-making, and a greater sense of purpose and direction.

We can create a more balanced and fulfilling life by embracing stillness and intentionality. We can respond to life's challenges more efficiently, build meaningful relationships, and find greater purpose and direction.

By cultivating this balance, we can experience a more profound sense of peace, connection, and fulfillment, leading to a more joyful and meaningful life.

The benefits of stillness and intentionality are numerous and can profoundly impact our overall well-being. By prioritizing these practices, we can experience a greater sense of calm, clarity, and purpose. We can become more aware of our thoughts, emotions, and actions and make more intentional choices that support our growth and well-being.

As we cultivate stillness and intentionality, we see the world in a new light. We can become more aware of the present moment and respond to situations with greater ease and composure. This increased awareness and clarity can lead to a more fulfilling and meaningful life and bring a sense of peace and contentment that we may have never experienced before.

The importance of stillness and intentionality cannot be overstated. We can experience more balance, clarity, and purpose by prioritizing these practices. We can become more aware of our thoughts, emotions, and actions and make more intentional choices that support our growth and well-being.

In today's fast-paced world, it can be easy to get caught up in the hustle and bustle of daily life. However, by prioritizing stillness and intentionality, we can create a sense of balance and harmony in our lives. We can become more aware of our thoughts, emotions, and actions and make more intentional choices that support our growth and well-being.

As we cultivate stillness and intentionality, we see the world in a new light. We can become more aware of the present moment and respond to situations with greater ease and composure. This increased awareness and clarity can lead to a more fulfilling and meaningful life and bring a sense of peace and contentment that we may have never experienced before.

We can create a more balanced and fulfilling life by embracing stillness and intentionality. We can respond to life's challenges more efficiently, build meaningful relationships, and find greater purpose and direction. By cultivating this balance, we can experience a more profound sense of peace, connection, and fulfillment, leading to a more joyful and meaningful life.

The benefits of stillness and intentionality are numerous and can profoundly impact our overall well-being. By prioritizing these practices, we can experience a greater sense of calm, clarity, and purpose. We can become more aware of our thoughts, emotions, and actions and make more intentional choices that support our growth and well-being.

The Path to Embodied Presence and Awareness

Cultivating mindfulness and presence allows us to connect deeply with ourselves and the present moment, shedding layers of distraction and unconscious patterns. Tuning into the physical body's sensations, movements, and rhythms develops a keen sense of embodied awareness, enhancing our capacity for presence and conscious living.

Practicing techniques to quiet the active mind, such as meditation, breath work, and other mindfulness practices, helps calm the mind's constant chatter, enabling a focused awareness. Embracing the power of sensory immersion by fully engaging the senses through activities like nature walks, art, or music can induce a state of flow and heightened presence.

One key aspect of cultivating embodied presence is developing self-awareness. This involves becoming more attuned to our thoughts, emotions, and physical sensations and learning to observe them without judgment. By doing so, we can begin to release patterns of self-criticism and self-doubt that often prevent us from feeling fully present.

Another essential component of embodied presence is self-compassion. When we practice self-compassion, we learn to treat ourselves with kindness, understanding, and patience, even amid challenges and difficulties. This helps us develop a greater sense of acceptance and love for ourselves, which is essential for cultivating a deep understanding of presence.

In addition to these internal practices, embracing sensory immersion is a powerful way to cultivate embodied presence. By engaging our senses more intentionally, we can tap into the natural world and allow ourselves to be fully present in the moment. For example, taking a slow and deliberate walk through nature and paying attention to the sights, sounds, and smells around us can be a powerful way to cultivate a sense of presence.

As we cultivate embodied presence, we begin to experience a greater sense of balance and harmony in our lives. We become more aware of our thoughts, emotions, and physical sensations and learn to navigate them with greater ease and awareness. We also become more present in our relationships, allowing us to connect with others on a deeper and more meaningful level.

TPracticingmindfulness and embodied presence is not a one-time achievement, but rather a continuous process of growth and development. It requires patience, kindness, and compassion and involves learning to listen to our bodies, honor our emotions, and cultivate a greater sense of awareness and presence.

By embracing the power of sensory immersion and cultivating a greater sense of awareness and presence, we can develop a greater understanding of balance and harmony in our lives. We can learn to navigate life's challenges with greater ease and clarity and to live more fully in the present moment.

In time, we can develop a greater sense of connection to ourselves and the world around us and live more intentionally and authentically. We can learn to appreciate the beauty of the present moment and find joy and meaning in the simplest of things.

As we continue cultivating embodied presence, we can develop greater self-awareness, self-acceptance, and self-compassion. We can learn to let go of our fears, doubts, and worries and to trust in our ability to navigate life's challenges with greater ease and confidence.

In the end, cultivating embodied presence is a journey that requires patience, kindness, and compassion. It involves learning to listen to our bodies, honor our emotions, and grow a greater sense of awareness and presence. By embracing this journey, we can better understand our connection to ourselves and the world and live more fully, intentionally, and authentically.

This process of growth and development can be challenging at times, but it is also gratifying. As we cultivate embodied presence, we can develop a greater sense of peace, happiness, and fulfillment. We can learn to live more fully in the present moment and find joy and meaning in the simplest things.

In time, we can develop a greater sense of balance and harmony and learn to navigate life's challenges more easily and clearly. We can learn to appreciate the beauty of the present moment and find joy and meaning in the simplest of things.

As we continue cultivating embodied presence, we can develop greater self-awareness, self-acceptance, and self-compassion. We can learn to let go of our fears, doubts, and worries and to trust in our ability to navigate life's challenges with greater ease and confidence.

By embracing the power of embodied presence, we can develop a greater sense of connection to ourselves and the world around us. We can learn to live more fully, intentionally, and authentically and find joy and meaning in the simplest things.

Cultivating embodied presence is a journey that requires patience, kindness, and compassion. It involves learning to listen to our bodies, honor our emotions, and grow a greater sense of awareness and presence. By embracing this journey, we can better understand our connection to ourselves and the world and live more fully, intentionally, and authentically.

As we cultivate embodied presence, we can develop a greater sense of balance and harmony. We can learn to navigate life's challenges with greater ease and clarity and to live more fully in the present moment.

In the end, cultivating embodied presence is a journey that requires patience, kindness, and compassion. It involves learning to listen to our bodies, honor our emotions, and grow a greater sense of awareness and presence. By embracing this journey, we can better understand our connection to ourselves and the world and live more fully, intentionally, and authentically.

By embracing the power of sensory immersion and cultivating a greater sense of awareness and presence, we can develop a greater understanding of balance and harmony in our lives. We can learn to navigate life's challenges with greater ease and clarity and to live more fully in the present moment.

As we continue cultivating embodied presence, we can develop self-awareness, self-acceptance, and self-compassion. We can learn to let go of our fears, doubts, and worries and rust in our ability to navigate life's challenges with greater ease and confidence.

In time, we can develop a greater sense of connection to ourselves and the world around us and live more fully, intentionally, and authentically. We can learn to appreciate the beauty of the present moment and find joy and meaning in the simplest of things.
As we cultivate embodied presence, we can develop a greater sense of balance and harmony. We can learn to navigate life's challenges with greater ease and clarity and to live more fully in the present moment.

In the end, cultivating embodied presence is a journey that requires patience, kindness, and compassion. It involves learning to listen to our bodies, honor our emotions, and grow a greater sense of awareness and presence. By embracing this journey, we can better understand our connection to ourselves and the world and live more fully, intentionally, and authentically.

This process of growth and development can be challenging at times, but it is also gratifying. As we cultivate embodied presence, we can develop a greater sense of peace, happiness, and fulfillment. We can learn to live more fully in the present moment and find joy and meaning in the simplest things.

By embracing the power of sensory immersion and cultivating a greater sense of awareness and presence, we can develop a greater understanding of balance and harmony in our lives. We can learn to navigate life's challenges with greater ease and clarity and to live more fully in the present moment.

As we continue cultivating embodied presence, we can develop greater self-awareness, self-acceptance, and self-compassion. We can learn to let go of our fears, doubts, and worries and to trust in our ability to navigate life's challenges with greater ease and confidence.

In time, we can develop a greater sense of connection to ourselves and the world around us and live more fully, intentionally, and authentically. We can learn to appreciate the beauty of the present moment and find joy and meaning in the simplest of things.

As we cultivate embodied presence, we can develop a greater sense of balance and harmony. We can learn to navigate life's challenges with greater ease and clarity and to live more fully in the present moment.

By embracing the power of embodied presence, we can develop a greater sense of connection to ourselves and the world around us. We can learn to live more fully, intentionally, and authentically and find joy and meaning in the simplest things.

Cultivating embodied presence is a journey that requires patience, kindness, and compassion. It involves learning to listen to our bodies, honor our emotions, and grow a greater sense of awareness and presence. By embracing this journey, we can better understand our connection to ourselves and the world and live more fully, intentionally, and authentically.

As we cultivate embodied presence, we can develop a greater sense of balance and harmony. We can learn to navigate life's challenges with greater ease and clarity and to live more fully in the present moment.

In the end, cultivating embodied presence is a journey that requires patience, kindness, and compassion. It involves learning to listen to our bodies, honor our emotions, and grow a greater sense of awareness and presence. By embracing this journey, we can better understand our connection to ourselves and the world and live more fully, intentionally, and authentically.

In time, we can develop a greater sense of connection to ourselves and the world around us and live more fully, intentionally, and authentically. We can learn to appreciate the beauty of the present moment and find joy and meaning in the simplest of things.

As we continue cultivating embodied presence, we can develop greater self-awareness, self-acceptance, and self-compassion. We can learn to let go of our fears, doubts, and worries and to trust in our ability to navigate life's challenges with greater ease and confidence.

By embracing the power of sensory immersion and cultivating a greater sense of awareness and presence, we can develop a greater understanding of balance and harmony in our lives. We can learn to navigate life's challenges with greater ease and clarity and to live more fully in the present moment.

As we cultivate embodied presence, we can develop a greater sense of balance and harmony. We can learn to navigate life's challenges with greater ease and clarity and to live more fully in the present moment.

Cultivating embodied presence is a journey that requires patience, kindness, and compassion. It involves learning to listen to our bodies, honor our emotions, and grow a greater sense of awareness and presence. By embracing this journey, we can better understand our connection to ourselves and the world and live more fully, intentionally, and authentically.

In the end, cultivating embodied presence is a journey that requires patience, kindness, and compassion. It involves learning to listen to our bodies, honor our emotions, and grow a greater sense of awareness and presence. By embracing this journey, we can better understand our connection to ourselves and the world and live more fully, intentionally, and authentically.

As we continue cultivating embodied presence, we can develop greater self-awareness, self-acceptance, and self-compassion. We can learn to let go of our fears, doubts, and worries and to trust in our ability to navigate life's challenges with greater ease and confidence.

By embracing the power of sensory immersion and cultivating a greater sense of awareness and presence, we can develop a greater understanding of balance and harmony in our lives. We can learn to navigate life's challenges with greater ease and clarity and to live more fully in the present moment.

As we cultivate embodied presence, we can develop a greater sense of balance and harmony. We can learn to navigate life's challenges with greater ease and clarity and to live more fully in the present moment.

In the end, cultivating embodied presence is a journey that requires patience, kindness, and compassion. It involves learning to listen to our bodies, honor our emotions, and cultivate greater awareness and presence. By embracing this journey, we can develop a greater sense of connection to ourselves and the world around us and live more fully, intentionally, and authentically.

This process of growth and development can be challenging at times, but it is also gratifying. As we cultivate embodied presence, we can develop a greater sense of peace, happiness, and fulfillment. We can learn to live more fully in the present moment and find joy and meaning in the simplest things.

By embracing the power of sensory immersion and cultivating a greater sense of awareness and presence, we can develop a greater understanding of balance and harmony in our lives. We can learn to navigate life's challenges with greater ease and clarity and to live more fully in the present moment.

As we continue cultivating embodied presence, we can develop greater self-awareness, self-acceptance, and self-compassion. We can learn to let go of our fears, doubts, and worries and to trust in our ability to navigate life's challenges with greater ease and confidence.

In time, we can develop a greater sense of connection to ourselves and the world around us and live more fully, intentionally, and authentically. We can learn to appreciate the beauty of the present moment and find joy and meaning in the simplest of things.

As we cultivate embodied presence, we can develop a greater sense of balance and harmony. We can learn to navigate life's challenges with greater ease and clarity and to live more fully in the present moment.

In the end, cultivating embodied presence is a journey that requires patience, kindness, and compassion. It involves learning to listen to our bodies, honor our emotions, and cultivate greater awareness and presence. By embracing this journey, we can develop a greater sense of connection to ourselves and the world around us and live more fully, intentionally, and authentically.

By embracing the power of sensory immersion and cultivating a greater sense of awareness and presence, we can develop a greater understanding of balance and harmony in our lives. We can learn to navigate life's challenges with greater ease and clarity and to live more fully in the present moment.

As we continue cultivating embodied presence, we can develop greater self-awareness, self-acceptance, and self-compassion. We can learn to let go of our fears, doubts, and worries and to trust in our ability to navigate life's challenges with greater ease and confidence.

In time, we can develop a greater sense of connection to ourselves and the world around us and live more fully, intentionally, and authentically. We can learn to appreciate the beauty of the present moment and find joy and meaning in the simplest of things.

As we cultivate embodied presence, we can develop a greater sense of balance and harmony. We can learn to navigate life's challenges with greater ease and clarity and to live more fully in the present moment.

By embracing the power of embodied presence, we can develop a greater sense of connection to ourselves and the world around us. We can learn to live more fully, intentionally, and authentically and find joy and meaning in the simplest things.

Chapter 2

Nature Immersion

Nature as a Teacher

Amid life's chaotic rhythm, it's easy to lose sight of what nourishes our minds, bodies, and spirits. We often find ourselves rushing from one task to the next, neglecting the subtle yet profound ways in which nature can soothe our frazzled nerves, calm our troubled minds, and revitalize our weary bodies. Yet, the natural world has always been a source of solace, comfort, and transformation, waiting to be rediscovered and explored.

As we embark on a journey to cultivate greater inner peace and well-being, we'll explore the transformative power of nature and its ability to restore balance and harmony to our lives. We'll delve into how immersing ourselves in the natural world can quiet the mind, soothe the senses, and promote a more profound understanding of connection to ourselves and the world around us. By embracing the healing power of nature, we can begin to let go of our burdens, quiet our worries, and reconnect with the present moment.

In the following pages, we'll discover the simple yet profound ways in which nature can become a source of strength, comfort, and inspiration. We'll explore the benefits of mindful observation, the therapeutic effects of outdoor spending, and how nature can help us cultivate a greater sense of presence, awareness, and inner peace. By doing so, we'll learn to navigate the complexities of modern life with greater ease, clarity, and confidence and discover the timeless wisdom that lies at the heart of nature's restorative power.

Immersing Ourselves in the Healing Power of Nature

Immersing ourselves in nature's restorative embrace can profoundly impact our mental and physical well-being. Engaging our senses with the natural world can calm our minds, soothe our senses, and promote inner peace. Whether observing the intricate beauty of a landscape, listening to the soothing sounds of flowing water, or inhaling the earthy scents of foliage, nature can induce a state of heightened presence.

The natural world is a whole of elements that can have a therapeutic effect on our bodies and minds. The grounding energy of the earth and the cleansing properties of water, air, and sunlight can all contribute to a sense of balance and harmony. By spending time outdoors, we can cultivate a deeper connection with the natural world and align ourselves with the rhythms and cycles of the environment.

One key benefit of immersing ourselves in nature is the opportunity to practice mindful observation. By slowing down and observing the world, we can enhance our awareness and appreciation of the present moment. This can be as simple as paying attention to nature's sights, sounds, and smells or as profound as recognizing the intricate web of relationships between living organisms and their environments.

In today's fast-paced world, it's easy to get caught up in the hustle and bustle of daily life. We often find ourselves rushing from one task to the next without taking the time to appreciate the beauty and wonder of the world around us. But by incorporating nature into our lives, we can begin to slow down and enjoy the simple things. We can start to see the world in a new light, as a place of beauty, wonder, and awe.

We can cultivate more profound inner peace and well-being by embracing nature's healing power. We can start to feel more grounded and connected to ourselves and the world around us. As we do, our lives become more intentional, more meaningful, and more fulfilling.

So take a deep breath, step outside, and immerse yourself in nature's restorative power. Allow yourself to be present in the moment and appreciate the beauty and wonder of the world around you. As you do, you may just find that you're better equipped to handle the challenges of everyday life with greater ease, confidence, and peace of mind.

The Healing Power of the Outdoors

The outdoors offers a unique sanctuary for the mind and spirit, providing an environment where individuals can reconnect with their inner selves and the world around them. Nature immersion encourages a deep sense of presence often lost in modern life's hustle. By stepping outside, one can experience the calming effects of the natural world, which has been shown to reduce stress, enhance mood, and foster a sense of belonging. The simplicity of natural settings allows for a profound engagement with the present moment, promoting mindfulness and an appreciation for the beauty surrounding us.

The outdoors is a powerful reminder of our values and priorities in the context of intentional living. Engaging with nature invites us to reflect on what truly matters, pushing aside distractions and societal expectations. When we immerse ourselves in natural environments, we are reminded of the interconnectedness of all living things.

This realization can inspire individuals to design their lives in alignment with their core beliefs, fostering a sense of purpose that transcends material concerns. As we cultivate a lifestyle that reflects our values, we find greater fulfillment and a more authentic expression of who we are.

The philosophy of non-action, or Wuwei, finds a natural application in outdoor experiences. By embracing being in nature, we learn to let go of the need for constant productivity and control. This flow state allows us to engage with the world without the pressure to achieve or accomplish.

Nature operates in its rhythm, teaching us the value of patience and the beauty of allowing things to unfold organically. In this way, the outdoors becomes a classroom for practicing non-action, where we can develop a deeper understanding of ourselves and our place within the more incredible tapestry of life.

Outdoor experiences enhance gratitude practices. Each moment spent in nature presents an opportunity to cultivate an appreciation for the wonders of life. Whether it is the gentle rustling of leaves, the vibrant colors of a sunset, or the intricate patterns of a flower, these elements remind us of the beauty inherent in our world.

Fostering acceptance through the lens of Amor Fati, or love of fate, allows us to embrace the present moment with open hearts. This gratitude enriches our outdoor experiences and permeates our daily lives, creating a more profound sense of contentment and joy.

Finally, the intersection of sustainable living and outdoor experiences encourages us to harmonize our lifestyle choices with the natural world. As we spend time in nature, we become more aware of the impact of our actions on the environment.

This awareness can drive meaningful change, prompting us to adopt practices that honor and protect the earth. By engaging with nature, we cultivate a sense of responsibility and stewardship, understanding that our well-being is intricately linked to the health of our surroundings. This connection fosters a more profound commitment to sustainability, encouraging us to live in ways that are not only beneficial to ourselves but also to future generations.

Mindfulness Practices in Natural Settings

Mindfulness practices in natural settings profoundly enhance one's awareness and presence. By immersing oneself in the natural world, individuals can cultivate a deep connection with their surroundings, fostering a sense of stillness often elusive in daily life.

Nature provides an ideal backdrop for these practices, as it encourages individuals to disengage from the distractions of modernity and reconnect with their inner selves. The gentle sounds of rustling leaves, flowing water, and distant bird calls create a soothing atmosphere that invites mindfulness, allowing individuals to engage fully with the present moment.

One effective mindfulness practice in nature is mindful walking. This practice involves paying close attention to each step taken, feeling the ground beneath one's feet, and observing the sensations in the body.

As one walks through a forest or along a beach, the rhythmic movement can serve as an anchor, drawing attention away from racing thoughts and redirecting it to the present moment. When done mindfully, this simple act of walking transforms the experience into a meditative journey that deepens one's appreciation for the beauty around them and enhances overall well-being.

Another powerful practice is using nature sounds for meditation. Individuals can cultivate a heightened sense of awareness by sitting quietly in a natural setting and focusing on ambient sounds—such as the chirping of birds, the rustle of grass, or the flow of water. This practice calms the mind and fosters an appreciation for the intricate symphony of life in the environment.

By actively listening, practitioners can develop a profound connection with the world around them, reinforcing that stillness and presence can be found in the simplest moments.

Incorporating gratitude into outdoor mindfulness practices further deepens the experience. Reflecting on what one is grateful for as one engages with nature can enhance feelings of contentment and acceptance.

This aligns with the philosophy of Amor Fati, or love of fate, where one learns to embrace life's circumstances with open arms. By acknowledging the beauty of nature and expressing gratitude for the experience, individuals can foster a more positive mindset and cultivate resilience against the stresses of modern life.

Finally, integrating a digital detox into mindfulness practices in nature can significantly amplify the benefits. Disconnecting from devices during outdoor experiences allows individuals to fully engage with their surroundings without the interruption of notifications or digital distractions.

This intentional living approach encourages participants to design their lives in alignment with their values, prioritizing presence and connection over constant connectivity. By embracing stillness in natural settings, individuals can find balance, cultivate awareness, and nurture a deeper relationship with themselves and the environment, ultimately leading to a more harmonious existence.

The Art of Mindful Walking and Its Connection to Stillness

Mindful walking is a powerful tool for cultivating presence and stillness. By directing one's full attention to the experience of each step, conscious walking creates a meditative state that anchors us in the present moment.

Connecting with nature through mindful walking heightens our sensory awareness and appreciation for the world around us. Immersing ourselves in natural environments while walking mindfully allows us to more deeply attune to the sights, sounds, and sensations of the present, fostering a sense of connection.

Mindful walking promotes a state of non-doing and non-striving, aligning with the principles of non-action. By allowing the body to move without attachment to the outcome, we cultivate a sense of effortless flow and presence, shedding the constant need to achieve or accomplish.
The rhythm and pace of mindful walking can induce a state of mental and physical calm. The steady grounding helps quiet the mind, reduce anxiety and restlessness, and enable a more profound inner peace and relaxation.

When we walk mindfully, we notice the subtle shifts in our surroundings, the changing light and shadow, the sounds of nature, and the texture of the ground beneath our feet. This heightened awareness allows us to appreciate the world's beauty, even during chaos.

Integrating mindful walking practices into daily life can foster better balance and presence. By making time for mindful walking, even in small increments, we can center ourselves and reconnect with the present amidst the busyness of daily life.

As we cultivate a greater sense of stillness and presence through mindful walking, we notice the intricate relationships between ourselves, nature, and the world around us. This newfound awareness can inspire a more profound sense of respect and compassion for all living beings and a renewed commitment to living in harmony with the natural world.

In a world that often values speed and productivity above all else, mindful walking offers a powerful antidote to the stresses and distractions of modern life. By slowing down and paying attention to the present moment, we can cultivate a sense of calm, clarity, and connection that brings us back to our true selves.

By incorporating mindful walking into our daily routine, we can experience the many benefits of this simple yet powerful practice, from reduced stress and anxiety to increased creativity and inspiration. So why not step in the right direction and see the transformative power of mindful walking?

Mindfulness and the art of stillness

Mindfulness and the art of stillness are intricately connected practices that invite us to reclaim our awareness amidst the often overwhelming chaos of everyday life. Mindfulness is a powerful tool that encourages us to anchor ourselves in the present moment. It invites us to engage fully with our thoughts, emotions, and physical sensations, offering a nonjudgmental space to observe our experiences as they unfold. This active engagement with the present enables us to cultivate a heightened level of awareness, creating a rich environment in which stillness can emerge.

Stillness, in this context, transcends the simple idea of silence or absence of activity. It represents a profound state of being—an inward journey where we can connect deeply with our core selves. This connection is essential as it nurtures a sense of inner peace, clarity, and balance, allowing us to understand our experiences and emotions better. By intentionally seeking moments of stillness amidst our hectic lives, we cultivate a sanctuary within ourselves, providing the space necessary for reflection and rejuvenation.

Deliberately slowing down and embracing quiet moments significantly benefits our mental and emotional well-being. In our fast-paced society, filled with distractions and responsibilities, the practice of stillness becomes our refuge. Returning from the relentless demands of modern existence fosters emotional resilience and enhances our mental clarity, allowing us to process our thoughts and feelings more effectively.

As we strive to integrate mindfulness and stillness into our daily routines, we embark on a transformative journey that significantly improves our overall well-being. This integration deepens our appreciation for each moment's beauty and simplicity, helping us recognize the extraordinary in the ordinary.

By embracing these interconnected practices, we empower ourselves to navigate life's complexities with grace and confidence, establishing a harmonious balance between dynamic action and restful repose. This balance enriches our lives, enabling us to face challenges with a calm and centered mindset, thus enhancing our overall quality of life.

Integrating Nature-Based Practices into Daily Life

As we navigate the complexities of modern life, it's easy to get caught up in the whirlwind of daily routines and lose touch with the natural world. However, incorporating nature-based practices into our daily lives can profoundly impact our well-being and sense of connection to the world around us.

Observing the changing seasons and natural cycles is one way to cultivate a deeper appreciation for nature. By paying attention to the rhythms of nature, we can develop a greater sense of awareness and presence in our lives. For example, noticing how the light changes throughout the day or how the trees change color with the seasons can be a powerful reminder of the impermanence of life.

Creating a nature-inspired space at home or work can also be a great way to stay grounded and connected to the natural world. This can be as simple as adding some plants to your workspace or bringing the outdoors in by using natural materials and colors in your decor. Even small changes can have a significant impact on our mood and productivity.

Engaging in outdoor physical activities is another excellent way to connect with nature and quiet the mind. Whether it's walking, hiking, or simply taking a few minutes to stretch outside, physical activity can help us feel more centered and connected to our surroundings. By combining physical activity with nature-based practices, we can experience many benefits, from improved physical health to greater well-being and happiness.

Finally, practicing gratitude for the natural world can be a powerful way to foster a more profound appreciation and connection to our surroundings. By taking a moment each day to reflect on the beauty and wonder of nature, we can cultivate a greater sense of gratitude and appreciation for the world around us.
This can be as simple as taking a few deep breaths outside or writing down three things you're grateful for daily. Incorporating nature-based practices into our daily lives can provide many benefits, from improved physical and mental health to a greater sense of connection and appreciation for the world around us.

Taking the time to appreciate the beauty of nature can also help us develop a greater sense of patience and understanding. As we slow down and pay attention to the natural world, we can see the intricate web of life surrounding us and the interconnectedness of all living things.

By living in greater harmony with nature, we can experience more excellent balance and well-being. We can learn to appreciate the simple things and find joy in the beauty of the world around us.

Incorporating nature-based practices into our daily lives can also help us develop a greater sense of compassion and empathy for all living things. As we cultivate a deeper appreciation for the natural world, we can see the world from a different perspective and develop a greater understanding and respect for the interconnectedness of all living things.

As we live in greater harmony with nature, we can experience greater peace and contentment. We can learn to appreciate the simple things and find joy in the beauty of the world around us. By incorporating nature-based practices into our daily lives, we can experience excellent balance, well-being, and connection to the world around us.

Cultivating stillness in daily life

Cultivating stillness in daily life is not merely a practice; it can serve as a transformative journey that significantly enhances our overall well-being and fosters a deeper connection with ourselves. Beginning this journey requires intentionality in carving out deliberate, quiet moments amidst our often hectic routines.

These moments can be achieved through meditation, focusing our minds and cultivating awareness, or mindful breathing exercises that anchor us to the present moment. Additionally, setting aside just a few minutes each day for silence—where we sit without distraction and allow our thoughts to settle—can create an oasis of tranquility in our busy lives.

Incorporating these practices regularly allows us to step back from the chaos that fills our days. By creating a space for reflection, we can experience clarity of thought and heightened emotional awareness. This intentional pause in our routine recharges our mental and emotional batteries and helps us recognize patterns and feelings that might go unnoticed.

Moreover, integrating mindful rituals into our daily activities can enrich our experience of stillness and significantly enhance our quality of life. For instance, during meals, instead of rushing through the process, we can take the time to truly focus on the flavors, aromas, and textures of our food. This practice fosters a sense of gratitude and presence, transforming an everyday activity into a sacred moment of appreciation.

Nature walks provide another excellent opportunity to invite stillness into our lives. When we intentionally engage with the beauty of our surroundings, we can observe the sights, sounds, and sensations without the distraction of technology or bustling thoughts. These walks are potent reminders of the peace in simplicity and mindfulness.

By embracing these habits and integrating them into our lives, we gradually cultivate an ongoing sense of calm that permeates all aspects of our existence. This cultivated calm helps us navigate the complexities of modern living with grace and intention, allowing us to respond to challenges with a serene demeanor and a clearer mind. Cultivating stillness can enhance clarity, deeper self-connection, and a more fulfilling life experience.

The path to authentic living

The path to authentic living is an intricate and transformative journey of self-discovery and alignment. It begins with a profound inner exploration, where individuals diligently ask themselves critical questions about what genuinely matters in their lives. This quest invites us to delve deep into our histories, experiences, and emotions, encouraging us to confront our innermost desires and fears.

Through this process, we gradually learn to differentiate between our aspirations and those imposed on us by societal expectations or external pressures, which frequently shape our choices without conscious awareness.

As we embark on this journey, we are called to shed the layers of conditioning that may have obscured our true identities. This shedding process can be liberating, allowing us to embrace our unique selves fully. We begin to cultivate self-awareness, developing a clearer understanding of our values, passions, and beliefs. This newfound clarity is the foundation upon which we can build a genuine and fulfilling life where our actions resonate deeply with our authentic selves.

Authentic living transcends merely representing our true selves; it involves a conscious commitment to integrate this authenticity into our daily interactions. It requires us to engage in intentionality, ensuring that every decision aligns with our core beliefs and values. This alignment creates a seamless connection between who we are internally and how we present ourselves externally, fostering a sense of integrity and inner peace.

We often experience a profound sense of purpose and fulfillment as we align our lives with our true selves. This alignment enriches our personal lives and enhances our resilience in navigating the complexities of daily life. Grounding ourselves in authenticity cultivates well-being, making us better equipped to face challenges and uncertainties confidently and gracefully.

Ultimately, the path to authentic living is a significant commitment to embracing vulnerability and being open to experiencing life in its fullest sense. It invites us to celebrate our individuality and honor the diverse journeys that each of us undertakes. As we engage in this process, we foster a life rich in meaning and connection, nurturing relationships that reflect our true selves and contribute to a sense of community. This authentic existence transforms our lives and inspires those around us, creating a ripple effect that encourages others to embark on their journeys of self-discovery.

Creating Outdoor Rituals for Presence

Creating outdoor rituals for presence involves intentional practices that foster a deep connection with nature, facilitating a state of mindfulness and awareness. To begin this journey, individuals can establish regular outdoor activities that anchor their experiences in the natural world. These rituals can be as simple as daily walks in a nearby park, organizing moonlit gatherings with friends, or creating a quiet space in the garden for reflection.

Each activity reminds participants to pause and engage fully with the environment, immersing them in the sights, sounds, and sensations surrounding them. By consistently engaging in these rituals, individuals cultivate a habit of presence that can be integrated into all aspects of life.

The practice of observation enhances mindfulness in nature. Setting aside time to observe the changing seasons, the behavior of local wildlife, or the intricate details of plants can deepen one's appreciation for the interconnectedness of life. This practice encourages a state of non-action, where individuals learn to be rather than do simply.

This aligns with the philosophy of wuwei, which emphasizes effortless action and flowing with the natural rhythms of the environment. Observing without judgment or the urge to control can develop a profound sense of peace and acceptance, which is essential for fostering daily gratitude and resilience.

Incorporating elements of intentional living can also enrich rituals. Participants can design their outdoor experiences to reflect their values, whether through sustainable practices like foraging, gardening, or engaging in community clean-up efforts.

These activities promote environmental stewardship and create a sense of belonging and purpose. When individuals align their outdoor rituals with their core values, they reinforce their commitment to living authentically and meaningfully. This alignment is a powerful reminder of the importance of making conscious choices that resonate with one's identity and aspirations.

Digital detoxification is another critical aspect of creating outdoor rituals for presence. In an age where connectivity often detracts from real-world experiences, setting boundaries around technology use can significantly enhance one's ability to engage with nature.

Establishing specific times for outdoor activities, free from digital distractions, allows individuals to immerse themselves fully in their surroundings. Whether it's a phone-free hike or a tech-free evening spent under the stars, these moments of disconnection can lead to greater clarity and insight. Embracing stillness in nature fosters a deeper appreciation for the present moment, allowing individuals to reconnect with themselves and the world around them.

Creating outdoor rituals for presence is a personal journey that invites exploration and adaptation. Individuals are encouraged to experiment with various practices, finding what resonates with them while keeping an open mind.

Whether through solitary reflection, communal gatherings, or nature-based activities, the goal remains to cultivate a sense of stillness and awareness. By embracing the philosophy of non-action and allowing nature to guide their experiences, individuals can develop a profound connection to themselves and their environment, fostering a life of balance and fulfillment.

Chapter 3

Intentional Living

Defining Personal Values

Defining personal values is a foundational exercise that empowers individuals to navigate the complexities of modern life with clarity and intention. Personal values represent the principles and beliefs that guide our choices, influence our behavior, and shape our identity. For independent-minded individuals, understanding these values is crucial to living authentically and aligning daily actions with more profound convictions.

This alignment is particularly significant in intentional living, where choices become expressions of what truly matters to us rather than mere reactions to external pressures or societal expectations.

To define personal values, one might begin by reflecting on pivotal moments that sparked joy, contentment, or fulfillment. These experiences often illuminate what we cherish most: relationships, creativity, adventure, or connection to nature. Engaging with these memories can help reveal underlying values that the hustle of daily life might have overshadowed.

Nature immersion plays a vital role in this discovery process. The tranquility and beauty of the outdoors can foster a profound sense of presence, allowing for introspection and clarity that might be elusive in more chaotic settings.

Once identified, personal values serve as a compass, guiding decisions and actions. They help individuals prioritize their time and energy toward endeavors that resonate with their core beliefs.

This is particularly relevant in sustainable living, where choices about consumption, conservation, and lifestyle can become more evident when grounded in one's values. By harmonizing lifestyle choices with nature and personal ethics, individuals can create a life that reflects their commitment to personal integrity and environmental stewardship.

The philosophy of non-action, or wuwei, emphasizes the importance of aligning with the natural flow of life rather than forcing outcomes. This philosophy can be intertwined with defining and adhering to personal values.

When individuals understand their values, they can approach life easily, making choices that feel more natural and less contrived. This can lead to a more meaningful existence, where actions are taken not out of obligation but as authentic expressions of who we are and what we stand for.

Finally, cultivating gratitude through practices such as amor fati—accepting one's fate—can further enrich the definition of personal values. Embracing our life experiences, both positive and negative, allows us to appreciate the lessons learned and the values forged through adversity.

This acceptance nurtures resilience and fosters a deeper understanding of what is truly significant in our lives. In defining personal values, the interplay of gratitude, presence, and intentionality creates a robust framework for living a balanced and fulfilling life amidst the distractions of the modern world.

Aligning Daily Actions with Values

Aligning daily actions with values is crucial to living an intentional life, especially for those who seek to cultivate presence and harmony through their choices. To truly embody the principles of deliberate living, individuals must first identify their core values. This process requires reflection and honesty, as understanding what truly matters gives a clearer vision of daily life.

Engaging in nature immersion can create a serene environment conducive to introspection, facilitating a deeper connection to personal values. In moments of stillness, the mind can sift through distractions, revealing what is essential and aligning actions with these insights.

Once core values are identified, the next step is to translate these values into actionable steps. This translation may involve setting specific, achievable goals that resonate with one's principles. For instance, if sustainability is a core value, daily actions might include walking instead of driving, participating in local environmental initiatives, or reducing waste at home. Such decisions reflect personal values and contribute collectively towards a healthier planet.

The philosophy of non-action, or wuwei, encourages individuals to align their actions naturally with their values rather than forcing change. This approach fosters a sense of ease, making incorporating meaningful practices into everyday life more straightforward.

Gratitude practices also play a vital role in aligning actions with values. Cultivating gratitude enhances awareness of what is truly important, allowing individuals to appreciate the small moments that embody their values.

By embracing amor fati—the love of one's fate—, individuals can develop acceptance of their circumstances while remaining open to growth and change. This acceptance creates fertile ground for aligning daily actions with values, as it encourages a mindset that seeks meaning in every experience.

Such practices can be woven into daily routines through journaling, meditation, or mindful walks in nature, reinforcing the connection to one's more profound principles. Digital detox strategies can further support the alignment of values and actions. In a world increasingly dominated by screens and notifications, disconnecting from digital distractions allows for greater clarity and focus on what truly matters.

By intentionally reducing time spent on social media or consuming information that does not enrich one's life, individuals can create space for reflection and engagement with their core values. This slower, more mindful approach fosters a deeper connection to oneself and the natural world, reinforcing the principles of sustainable living and intentionality.

Ultimately, aligning daily actions with values requires self-awareness and ongoing reflection. It is a practice that evolves, requiring individuals to regularly assess their choices and ensure they resonate with their true selves.

By integrating the concepts of nature immersion, gratitude, and wuwei into daily life, individuals can cultivate a lifestyle that reflects their values and contributes to a more meaningful existence. This conscious alignment enhances personal fulfillment and resonates outward, creating a ripple effect that can inspire others to engage in their journeys toward intentional living.

The Impact of Intentional Choices on Well-Being

Intentional choices are a foundation for enhancing well-being, intertwining individual values with everyday actions. In a world rife with distractions and rapid changes, the ability to make deliberate decisions becomes essential in cultivating a life that resonates with one's true self. This process begins with self-awareness, allowing individuals to recognize what genuinely matters to them.

People can align their choices with a broader purpose by prioritizing their values, leading to a more fulfilling existence. This alignment fosters a sense of coherence and direction, contributing significantly to overall well-being.

Engaging with nature provides an ideal context for practicing intentionality. Nature immersion not only invites individuals to disconnect from the noise of modern life but also encourages reflection on personal values. Spending time outdoors can cultivate presence and allow one to experience the serenity of fully engaging with the environment.

This connection to nature prompts individuals to consider their choices more thoughtfully, recognizing how each decision impacts their lives and the ecosystem around them. Such experiences can reshape priorities, steering individuals toward sustainable living practices that honor personal and environmental health.

The philosophy of non-action, or wuwei, emphasizes the power of being rather than doing. This concept challenges the relentless pursuit of productivity that often overshadows thoughtful decision-making. By embracing wuwei, individuals can foster a mindset that values stillness and contemplation.

This approach encourages considering how each action aligns with one's values, leading to choices that contribute positively to personal well-being. In doing so, people can learn to appreciate moments of pause, allowing their intentions to guide them rather than the demands of external pressures.

Incorporating gratitude practices into daily life also enhances the impact of intentional choices. By fostering an attitude of acceptance, individuals can shift their focus from what is lacking to what is present. This shift nurtures a deeper appreciation for the choices, reinforcing the connection between actions and values.

Such practices cultivate resilience, enabling individuals to face challenges with gratitude for the lessons learned. This perspective enhances well-being and encourages a more profound engagement with life, aligning actions with a mindset of abundance rather than scarcity.

Digital detoxification emerges as another crucial aspect of intentional living. In a hyper-connected world, the constant influx of information can overwhelm personal agency and clarity. Individuals can reclaim their time and mental space by deliberately disconnecting from digital distractions. This intentional pause allows for reflection on personal values and the choices that stem from them.

The resulting clarity can lead to a more meaningful life as individuals make decisions that resonate with their true selves rather than those shaped by external influences. Ultimately, embracing intentional choices fosters a more prosperous, balanced existence, harmonizing individual well-being with a deeper connection to the world.

The Impact of Intentional Choices on Wellbeing

Intentional choices shape our overall well-being, profoundly influencing our mental and physical health. We foster a more profound sense of purpose when we consciously align our actions with our core values and long-term aspirations.

This alignment enhances our day-to-day satisfaction and serves as a guiding force that encourages us to live more mindfully. By being more aware of our decisions, we can actively reflect on our choices rather than simply reacting to the external pressures and demands that often pull us in different directions.

For instance, making an effort to choose nourishing foods over quick and convenient meals can significantly impact our energy levels, mood, and overall health by dedicating time to self-care activities—whether physical exercise, meditation, or simply enjoying a quiet moment—we proactively enhance our emotional resilience.

Engaging in meaningful relationships is paramount; surrounding ourselves with supportive individuals fosters a sense of connection and belonging that is essential for our mental health.

The effects of these intentional choices extend far beyond our individual lives; they reverberate throughout our communities and the broader environment. Embracing sustainable practices, such as reducing waste, opting for eco-friendly products, and supporting local businesses, not only contributes to the health of our planet but also cultivates a sense of belonging and shared responsibility. Our mindful action resonates with others, encouraging a ripple effect that promotes community consciousness and environmental stewardship.

By weaving intentionality into the fabric of our daily lives, we adopt a holistic approach to well-being that nurtures not just ourselves but also the relationships we cherish and the world we inhabit. Such an approach recognizes the interconnectedness of our personal choices and their broader implications, positioning intentional choices as foundational to a fulfilling life. Ultimately, embodying clarity and purpose enables us to navigate the complexities of modern existence with grace, making every decision a step towards a more meaningful and enriched life.

Sustainable Living and the Art of Acceptance

Sustainable living transcends being merely a lifestyle choice; it embodies a profound commitment to nurturing a harmonious relationship with our planet and its invaluable resources. This philosophy encourages individuals to engage in mindful consumption, which means making intentional choices about what we buy and use, reducing waste, and placing a greater emphasis on practices that benefit our well-being and the health of the environment.

By adopting sustainable practices—be it shifting to renewable energy sources, supporting local economies, or reducing our carbon footprint—we have the potential to create a positive ripple effect that extends throughout our communities and influences generations to come.

Yet, the pursuit of sustainability has its challenges. It requires us to embrace the art of acceptance—a crucial component that encourages us to acknowledge the complexities and difficulties inherent in our efforts. This involves recognizing personal limitations, such as our time and resource constraints, and more enormous systemic obstacles, such as economic structures and societal norms that may hinder our progress. Acceptance is about finding peace in our aspirations to make a meaningful difference, even when the results of our efforts may not align with our expectations or ideals.

An essential aspect of this mindset is understanding that perfection is an unrealistic goal. By accepting this, we allow ourselves to take incremental steps toward sustainability, celebrating even the most minor victories.

Whether we reduce our plastic use, participate in community clean-ups, or simply adopt more eco-friendly habits at home, every action contributes to the greater goal of sustainability. This approach nurtures resilience, empowering us to persist in our values and efforts, even when faced with setbacks or challenges.

Integrating acceptance into our sustainable living practices fosters a more profound sense of purpose and fulfillment. It grounds us to understand that every effort, no matter how seemingly insignificant, plays a vital role in the broader narrative of environmental stewardship.

By shifting our focus from the idealized vision of a perfectly sustainable world to the practical realities of our journey, we cultivate a more meaningful engagement with our lifestyles and the planet. Ultimately, this blend of mindful action and acceptance transforms the journey toward sustainability into a collective mission that enriches our lives and the world around us.

The Connection Between Sustainability and Stillness

The intricate connection between sustainability and stillness is deeply rooted in the mindful awareness we nurture when we intentionally embrace non-action moments. In our increasingly fast-paced society, where the relentless demands of daily life often propel us into a cycle of mindless consumption, we frequently find ourselves disconnected from the natural world.

This disconnection can lead to hasty decisions that overlook our choices' profound implications on the environment. However, by incorporating stillness practices into our routines, we can cultivate a richer understanding and appreciation for the interconnectedness of all living beings, acknowledging the ripple effects our actions can have on the planet.

When we carve out time for stillness—whether through meditation, quiet reflection, or simply pausing to observe our surroundings—we open ourselves to gaining clarity on our values and intentions.

This clarity is crucial, as it empowers us to align our daily choices with sustainable practices that nurture our well-being and honor the Earth's ecosystems. In these moments of inner calm, we begin to recognize the significance of making mindful decisions, viewing our consumption through a lens of sustainability rather than immediacy.

Moreover, stillness facilitates a deeper reflection on the transient nature of the resources at our disposal and underscores the essential need for living in harmony with our environment. This reflective process can catalyze a profound shift in perspective, steering us away from the pursuit of immediate gratification and towards an appreciation for long-term solutions prioritizing ecological balance and stewardship.

As we dedicate ourselves to a practice of stillness, we gradually understand that sustainability transcends mere choices; it embodies a holistic mindset that influences how we approach life.

Grounding ourselves in stillness empowers us to adopt a thoughtful and intentional way of living that honors and respects the delicate web of life we are all inextricably part of. In this sense, stillness becomes not just a practice of pausing but a vital tool for transforming our relationship with the world around us, fostering a sustainable future for all.

The Importance of Gratitude and Acceptance in Sustainable Living

Gratitude and acceptance are fundamental components in nurturing a sustainable lifestyle. They foster a mindset that appreciates the environment, our communal relationships, and our role within the larger ecological framework. When we actively cultivate an attitude of gratitude, we develop a profound appreciation for the myriad resources provided by nature.

This includes the essentials like clean air and water, the scenic beauty surrounding us—lush forests, vibrant landscapes, and the diverse flora and fauna that inhabit our planet. Recognizing these treasures nurtures a sense of responsibility towards safeguarding our environment as we become more attuned to how our well-being is intricately linked to the health of the Earth.

In this context, gratitude is transformative; it compels us to reflect on our consumption patterns and encourages us to adopt more mindful practices. For instance, when we express gratitude for the food we eat, we may support local farmers, opt for organic produce, or reduce food waste, all of which are steps toward sustainability.

Each conscious choice we make as consumers can reflect our dedication to environmental stewardship and social responsibility, leading us to seek out more sustainable products and practices.

On the other hand, acceptance offers us the strength to recognize the limits of our control in a world burdened by pressing environmental challenges. It allows us to confront the harsh realities of climate change, pollution, and resource depletion without becoming overwhelmed.

Rather than striving for an unattainable standard of perfection, acceptance encourages us to embrace the idea that sustainable living is a continuous journey. This journey may be riddled with obstacles, failures, and setbacks, but it is also rich with opportunities for growth and learning.

Accepting our achievements and shortcomings builds resilience in our sustainability efforts. This mindset fosters a focus on small, incremental changes instead of drastic transformations, promoting a sense of gradual improvement and progress.

As we navigate this path of acceptance, we can cultivate a stronger sense of community among those who share our commitment to sustainability. Together, we can support each other in overcoming challenges and celebrating victories, creating a shared understanding of responsibility towards a healthier planet.

Ultimately, the intertwining concepts of gratitude and acceptance form a robust foundation for meaningful action. They empower us to live sustainably in our daily lives and deepen our connections with ourselves, our communities, and the natural world. As we embrace these principles, we are better equipped to contribute to a sustainable future that honors the delicate balance of our ecosystem while fostering a sense of belonging and purpose in our shared journey.

Chapter 4

Gratitude Practices

Cultivating a Culture of Gratitude

Gratitude is a powerful catalyst for transforming our lives. By focusing on the good things in our lives, we can shift our perspective, cultivate a more positive outlook, and experience many benefits beyond feeling happy and content. Research has shown that practicing gratitude can increase happiness, life satisfaction, and optimism while improving mental and physical well-being.

As we explore the benefits of gratitude, we'll delve into how it can help us manage difficult emotions, build stronger relationships, and improve our overall quality of life. From reducing stress and anxiety to fostering more profound connections with others, the impact of gratitude on our lives is profound and multifaceted. By incorporating gratitude into our daily routines, we can experience various benefits that can help us live a happier, healthier, and more fulfilling life.

In this section, we'll examine how gratitude can positively impact our lives, from improving our mental and physical health to strengthening our relationships and fostering a sense of community. We'll explore practical strategies for cultivating gratitude, including journaling, meditation, and simply reflecting on the good things in our lives each day.

The Benefits of Gratitude on Mental and Physical Health

Cultivating gratitude has been shown to impact mental and physical well-being profoundly. By shifting our focus from negative thoughts and worries, practicing gratitude helps us promote a calmer state of mind and reduce stress and anxiety. This, in turn, leads to better sleep, more muscular immune function, and lower blood pressure.

Studies have demonstrated that individuals who practice gratitude experience increased happiness, life satisfaction, and optimism. This is because gratitude helps us appreciate the good things in our lives, no matter how small they seem. By focusing on what we are thankful for, we see the world more positively and improve our overall outlook.

Gratitude also plays a significant role in fostering more profound, more meaningful relationships with others. We build stronger social connections and create a sense of community when we express genuine appreciation for those around us. This, in turn, can lead to increased feelings of belonging and reduced loneliness.
In addition to its benefits for mental and emotional well-being, practicing gratitude has also improved physical health. By reducing stress and anxiety, gratitude can help lower blood pressure, enhance sleep quality, and boost our immune system.

One key benefit of gratitude is its ability to help us manage difficult emotions and respond to challenges with resilience. When we focus on what we are grateful for, we see challenges as opportunities for growth and learning rather than threats to our well-being. This allows us to approach life's challenges calmly and confidently rather than with fear and anxiety.

By incorporating gratitude into our daily lives, we can experience many benefits that extend far beyond just feeling happy and content. We can build stronger relationships, improve physical health, and develop the resilience to navigate life's challenges easily. Whether we express gratitude through journaling, meditation, or simply taking a moment to reflect on the good things in our lives, the impact can be profound and lasting.

Incorporating gratitude into our daily routine can be as simple as reflecting on the good things that have happened daily. This can be as easy as writing in a gratitude journal, sharing three things we are thankful for with a friend or family member, or simply taking a moment to pause and appreciate the good things in our lives. By making gratitude a regular part of our daily routine, we can experience various benefits that can help us live a happier, healthier, and more fulfilling life.

Effective Strategies for Practicing Gratitude

Establishing a daily gratitude practice can profoundly impact our mindset and overall outlook on life. We can cultivate a more positive and appreciative attitude by dedicating a few minutes each day to reflecting on things we are grateful for. Keeping a gratitude journal is one way to make this practice more tangible. Writing down specific things we are thankful for, even in simple bullet point form, can help us track our progress over time and provide a sense of accomplishment.

Reframing challenging situations can also be a powerful way to cultivate gratitude. By trying to find the hidden blessings or lessons learned from a challenging experience, we can shift our perspective to appreciation. This can help us to see the world in a more positive light and to find opportunities for growth and learning.

Expressing gratitude to others is another crucial aspect of cultivating gratitude. Verbalizing our appreciation to friends, family, and strangers can brighten someone's day and strengthen our relationships. It can also help us to develop a greater sense of empathy and compassion for others.

Engaging in gratitude-focused activities can also deepen our connection to the practice and foster a shared appreciation. Participating in gratitude-based meditations, rituals, or community gatherings can provide a sense of community and support and help us stay motivated and inspired in our gratitude practice.

By incorporating these practices into our daily lives, we can develop tremendous gratitude and appreciation for the world around us. We can learn to see the beauty and wonder in everyday experiences and to find joy and meaning in the simple things. We can live more intentional, mindful, and fulfilling lives by cultivating gratitude.

In addition to its benefits, cultivating gratitude can positively impact our relationships and community. By expressing gratitude to others, we can build stronger, more meaningful connections with those around us. By engaging in gratitude-focused activities, we can come together with others to share the gratitude experience and support one another.

Cultivating gratitude requires intention and effort, but the rewards can be significant. By prioritizing gratitude, we can create a more positive and supportive environment for ourselves and those around us. This, in turn, can lead to greater happiness, well-being, and fulfillment.

By making gratitude a regular part of our lives, we can experience its many benefits and live more joyfully and meaningfully. Ultimately, cultivating gratitude is a process that takes time and practice, but it can have a profound impact on our lives.

By incorporating gratitude into our daily lives, we can develop a greater appreciation and wonder for the world around us and live more intentional, mindful, and fulfilling lives. By cultivating gratitude, we can create a more positive and supportive environment and experience its many benefits.

The Connection Between Gratitude and Acceptance

Gratitude and acceptance are intricately linked, with gratitude catalyzing acceptance. By cultivating gratitude, we open ourselves to a more optimistic outlook on life, becoming more inclined to acknowledge the joys and challenges that come our way. This mindset shift allows us to release resistance, freeing us from constant striving and struggle.

When we practice gratitude, we develop a more compassionate understanding of ourselves and our circumstances, including their imperfections. This self-acceptance enables us to focus on what truly nourishes us rather than expending energy on the need for control. Doing so makes us more at peace, present, and fulfilled.

The synergy between gratitude and acceptance creates a harmonious effect, allowing us to live more efficiently and simply. We let go of unnecessary stress and anxiety by embracing the present moment and cultivating a deeper appreciation for life's beauty. This harmony also empowers us to make intentional choices, aligning our actions with our values and priorities.

Gratitude and acceptance are not mutually exclusive; instead, they work in tandem to profoundly impact our well-being. By acknowledging the good in our lives, we become more inclined to accept life as it is, with all its imperfections and uncertainties.

This acceptance allows us to focus on what truly matters rather than getting caught up in resistance and struggle. Incorporating gratitude and acceptance into our daily lives can be as simple as taking a few moments each day to reflect on what we're thankful for.

This practice can be as informal as jotting down three things we appreciate or as structured as participating in a regular reflection routine. Whatever the approach, the key is to cultivate a mindset that acknowledges the beauty and complexity of life and approaches challenges with a sense of openness and curiosity.

By embracing the interconnectedness of gratitude and acceptance, we can cultivate a more profound sense of peace, presence, and fulfillment. This harmony enables us to live more intentionally, making choices that align with our values and priorities. In doing so, we can create a more balanced and fulfilling life, one that is marked by a deep appreciation for the beauty and complexity of existence.

The Concept of Amor Fati

Amor Fati, a Latin phrase meaning "love of fate," encapsulates the profound acceptance of all life experiences, both positive and negative. This concept encourages individuals to embrace their circumstances with gratitude and resilience. For those who find solace in nature immersion, Amor Fati aligns perfectly with the principles of being present in the moment. When immersed in the natural world, one learns to appreciate the unfolding of experiences without needing control or judgment.

Nature teaches us that every season, challenge, and beauty is integral to the larger tapestry of life, urging us to cultivate an appreciation for what is rather than what we wish it to be.

In the context of intentional living, Amor Fati invites individuals to design their lives in alignment with personal values while accepting the unpredictability of existence. Rather than resisting life's challenges, embracing them can lead to more profound personal growth and fulfillment.

This acceptance fosters a sense of peace, allowing one to navigate life authentically. By recognizing that every setback or unexpected event has a purpose, individuals can curate lives that reflect their true selves without the burden of resistance to circumstances beyond their control.

The philosophy of non-action, or Wuwei, complements the idea of Amor Fati by promoting a state of effortless action rooted in alignment with the natural flow of life. In practicing Wuwei, individuals learn to respond to life's challenges without force, allowing situations to unfold as they must. This aligns with the concept of loving one's fate, as it encourages a mindset that trusts in the process of life. By letting go of the need to control outcomes, one can engage with life more fully, experiencing richness and depth in each moment, much like how one might appreciate the changing colors of leaves in autumn.

Gratitude practices are essential in fostering acceptance and embodying Amor Fati. By regularly acknowledging the lessons and gifts that arise from joyful and challenging experiences, individuals can cultivate a mindset that embraces life.

This practice enhances emotional well-being and strengthens the ability to remain present. When gratitude becomes a habit, it reshapes one's perspective, allowing for a deeper understanding of life's inherent value and interconnectedness. It parallels the lessons learned through immersing oneself in the natural world.

Finally, Amor Fati is a guiding principle for creating a slower, more meaningful life in digital detox and sustainable living. Disconnecting from the constant noise of the digital world enables individuals to reconnect with their surroundings and authentic selves.

Embracing one's fate naturally leads to more conscientious lifestyle choices harmonizing with nature's rhythms. By fostering a sense of acceptance of life's ebbs and flows, individuals can cultivate a lifestyle that is not only sustainable but deeply fulfilling, honoring both the earth and their journey.

Daily Gratitude Exercises

Daily gratitude exercises are powerful tools for cultivating presence and enhancing our connection to the world around us. For those engaged in nature immersion, intentional living, and the philosophy of non-action, these practices can deepen one's appreciation for the subtleties of life.

By acknowledging the beauty in everyday moments, we foster a sense of acceptance and harmony that aligns with personal values and broader ecological principles. In this context, gratitude becomes a fleeting emotion and a sustained practice that enriches our interactions with nature and ourselves.

One effective daily gratitude exercise is mindful observation. This involves spending a few moments each day in a natural setting, whether in a park, a garden, or a quiet corner of your backyard. As you immerse yourself in the environment, take note of the details—the colors of the leaves, the sounds of birds, the texture of the ground beneath your feet.

Allow yourself to fully experience these sensations, expressing gratitude for the simple beauty surrounding you. This practice heightens your awareness and reinforces the connection between your values and the natural world, encouraging an intentional and sustainable lifestyle.

Another exercise involves journaling, where individuals can dedicate time each morning or evening to reflect on what they are grateful for. This can include specific experiences, interactions, or challenges contributing to personal growth. By writing down these thoughts, you create a tangible record of appreciation that serves as a reminder of the abundance in your life.

This habit aligns seamlessly with the philosophy of non-action, as it emphasizes an internal shift in perception rather than striving for external achievements. The act of gratitude becomes a form of stillness, allowing us to embrace moments of reflection and acceptance.

Integrating gratitude into daily routines can also be achieved through intentional moments of appreciation during ordinary activities. For instance, while cooking, take a moment to express gratitude for the ingredients, their origins, and the nourishment they provide. By consciously acknowledging the effort involved in these mundane tasks, you cultivate presence and transform routine into a sacred practice.

This approach enriches your daily life and harmonizes your actions with the principles of sustainable living, emphasizing a mindful consumption that respects the earth's resources.

Lastly, digital detoxification can enhance gratitude practices by reducing distractions and fostering deeper connections with the present moment. Designate specific times to disconnect from technology, allowing space for reflection and appreciation of your surroundings. During these intervals, engage in activities such as walking in nature, meditating, or sitting silently.

This not only cultivates a sense of stillness but also amplifies your capacity for gratitude as you become more attuned to the nuances of life that often go unnoticed amidst the noise of modern living. By embracing these daily gratitude exercises, you align your life more closely with your values, fostering a deeper connection to yourself and the world around you.

Daily Gratitude Exercises

Gratitude is a powerful practice that can significantly enhance our mental and emotional wellbeing. Daily gratitude exercises help shift our focus from what we lack to appreciating what we have, fostering a more positive outlook on life. Here are several practical gratitude exercises to incorporate into your daily routine:

1. Gratitude Journaling

Set aside a few minutes each day to write in a gratitude journal. List three to five things you are grateful for that day. They can be significant, like a promotion at work, or tiny, like a delicious meal. This practice helps you focus on positivity and encourages reflection on your daily experiences.

2. Gratitude Prompts

If you find it challenging to get started, consider using gratitude prompts. Each day, reflect on a question such as:

- What made me smile today?
- Who is someone I appreciate in my life, and why?
- What is something I often take for granted?

Answering these prompts can deepen your gratitude practice and offer new insights into your life.

3. Gratitude Jar

Create a gratitude jar to represent your thankfulness visually. Write short notes about things you are grateful for on slips of paper and place them in the jar throughout the year. When you're feeling down, revisit the jar and read the notes to remind yourself of your life's positive aspects.

4. Gratitude Meditation

Set aside time for a gratitude meditation. Find a quiet space, close your eyes, and take deep breaths. Focus on the people, experiences, and things you are grateful for. Visualize each one and allow the feelings of gratitude to wash over you. This mindfulness practice can enhance your emotional well-being and increase your awareness of positive experiences.

5. **Expressing Gratitude to Others**
Make it a habit to express your gratitude to the people in your life. Whether through a heartfelt note, a text, or a face-to-face conversation, acknowledging others' contributions fosters connection and strengthens relationships. Consider choosing one person each day to tell them how much you appreciate them.

6. **Gratitude Walks**
Take gratitude walks to combine physical activity with mindfulness. As you walk, focus on the beauty of your surroundings and the positive elements of your life. With each step, mentally acknowledge something you are grateful for, whether it's nature, your health, or your loved ones.

7. **Gratitude Visualization**
Spend a few minutes visualizing moments that bring you joy or comfort. Imagine the details, such as the sights, sounds, and feelings associated with those experiences. This practice helps reinforce positive memories and cultivates a sense of gratitude in your everyday life.

8. **Celebrate the Small Wins**
At the end of each day, reflect on your small victories—no matter how minor they may seem. Whether it's completing a task you had been procrastinating on or simply making time for self-care, acknowledging these moments can help reinforce a positive mindset.

Incorporating these daily gratitude exercises into your routine can lead to profound shifts in your perspective. By consistently practicing gratitude, you cultivate a habit of positivity, resilience, and appreciation, enhancing your overall quality of life.

Fostering Acceptance Through Reflection

Fostering acceptance through reflection is an essential practice that intertwines the principles of stillness with the art of introspection. As independent-minded individuals navigate their lives, the ability to pause and reflect becomes a powerful tool for understanding oneself and the surrounding environment.

Reflection encourages an exploration of personal values and beliefs, enabling individuals to align their actions with their true selves. This process fosters acceptance by allowing individuals to confront their thoughts and emotions non-judgmentally, creating a foundation for deeper connections with themselves and the world around them.

Nature immersion is a perfect backdrop for reflection, offering a serene environment that enhances the contemplative process. Engaging with the natural world invites a sense of presence, allowing individuals to step away from the distractions of modern life.

The sounds of rustling leaves, the sight of flowing water, and the feel of the earth beneath one's feet can anchor the mind, making it easier to delve into personal thoughts and feelings. This immersion cultivates a space where acceptance can flourish as individuals learn to appreciate the beauty and complexity of their positive and negative experiences.

Intentional living further emphasizes the importance of reflection to foster acceptance. Individuals create a framework for understanding their choices and actions by designing a life that aligns with personal values.

This intentionality requires a reflective mindset to assess whether current pursuits resonate with their core beliefs. Such reflection promotes acceptance of one's current situation and encourages a proactive approach to future decisions, allowing for growth and adaptability in facing life's uncertainties.

The philosophy of non-action, particularly the concept of wuwei, complements reflective practices by encouraging a state of flow and ease. Embracing non-action does not imply passivity; instead, it emphasizes the importance of aligning with the natural rhythms of life.

Through reflective observation, individuals can identify when to exert effort and when to let go, fostering a sense of acceptance regarding the outcomes of their actions. This balance between action and stillness cultivates resilience, enabling individuals to embrace the unfolding of life without resistance.

Gratitude practices, particularly the concept of amor fati, further enhance acceptance through reflection. Individuals learn to appreciate every experience as a vital part of their journey by cultivating a mindset that embraces fate. Reflecting on challenges and setbacks through gratitude fosters a deeper understanding of their significance, transforming potential obstacles into opportunities for growth.

This shift in perspective enriches personal acceptance and nurtures a harmonious relationship with nature and the broader world, reinforcing the interconnectedness of all experiences.

Integrating Gratitude into Daily Life and Rituals

Incorporating gratitude into daily life can profoundly impact our well-being and relationships. One effective way to cultivate gratitude is by keeping a gratitude journal. By writing down a few sentences each day about what we're thankful for, we can develop a deeper appreciation for the positive aspects of our lives. This simple practice can help us stay present and focused on the good things rather than getting caught up in worries about the future or regrets about the past.

Another way to integrate gratitude into daily routines is to make it a habit to express thanks during meals, before bedtime, or when starting the day. This can be as simple as sharing a few words of appreciation with family or friends or reflecting on the blessings in our lives. By weaving gratitude into our daily activities, we can cultivate a mindset of thankfulness and positively impact those around us.

Mindfulness exercises, such as meditation, can also be powerful tools for cultivating gratitude. By dedicating time to focus on the present moment and letting go of distractions, we can deepen our connection to the world and appreciate its beauty and wonder. We can tune into the subtle shifts in our energy and perspective when we are still and quiet.

Sharing gratitude with others can also be a powerful way to strengthen relationships and spread positivity. By expressing thanks to loved ones, we can create a sense of connection and community and show that we value and appreciate them. Whether it's a kind word, a thoughtful gesture, or a simple act of service, showing gratitude to others can impact our relationships and the world around us.

Even in household tasks, we can find ways to cultivate gratitude. By focusing on the simple joys of everyday life, such as the beauty of nature or the comfort of a warm home, we can transform mundane activities into opportunities for mindfulness and connection. By incorporating gratitude into all aspects of our lives, we can create a more balanced and fulfilling existence and appreciate the beauty and wonder of the world around us.

Chapter 5

The Philosophy of Non-Action

An Introduction to Wuwei

An introduction to the concept of Wuwei reveals a profound philosophy rooted in the principles of Taoism. Wuwei, often translated as "non-action" or "effortless action," invites individuals to embrace a state of being that transcends the frenetic pace of modern life.

In essence, Wuwei encourages a harmonious existence, where actions are aligned with the natural flow of life rather than imposed through force or struggle. This approach resonates deeply with those seeking to cultivate presence and awareness, particularly within nature immersion and intentional living.

The practice of Wuwei emphasizes the importance of aligning oneself with the rhythms of the natural world. By observing how nature operates without unnecessary exertion, individuals can learn to recognize the value of stillness and patience.

This perspective can be incredibly enlightening for those engaged in outdoor experiences, where immersion in nature fosters a deeper connection to the environment. Wuwei's insights encourage individuals to trust their instincts, allowing for a more authentic and meaningful interaction with the world around them.

Regarding personal values and intentional living, Wuwei is a guiding principle for designing a life that reflects one's true self. It invites individuals to assess their choices through the lens of alignment rather than ambition.

By embracing non-action, one can cultivate a sense of grace and ease, making decisions that resonate with inner desires rather than external pressures. This philosophy fosters a deeper understanding of living authentically, encouraging a fulfilling and sustainable lifestyle.

Furthermore, Wuwei intersects beautifully with gratitude practices, particularly the concept of Amor Fati—the love of fate. Embracing Wuwei allows individuals to accept their circumstances without resistance, fostering a sense of gratitude for the present moment.

This acceptance nurtures resilience and encourages a mindset that finds beauty in the unfolding of life's journey. By relinquishing the need for control, individuals can cultivate a profound appreciation for their experiences, grounding themselves in the present and fostering a deeper connection to their surroundings.

Finally, in an age dominated by digital distractions, Wuwei offers a refreshing perspective on disconnecting from technology to create space for reflection and presence. The philosophy of non-action advocates for intentional pauses, which can lead to a more meaningful and balanced life.

By harmonizing lifestyle choices with the principles of Wuwei, individuals can navigate the complexities of modern living with a sense of calm and clarity. This alignment enhances personal well-being and fosters a sustainable relationship with nature, encouraging a lifestyle that honors self and environment.

Historical Context and Relevance

The concept of stillness has deep historical roots that transcend cultures and eras, shaping philosophical, spiritual, and practical approaches to life. Ancient practices, particularly within Eastern traditions, emphasize the importance of non-action, or wuwei, to achieve harmony with the natural world and inner peace.

This principle advocates for a state of effortless action, where individuals align themselves with the rhythms of nature rather than striving against them. In this context, stillness is not simply the absence of movement but a profound engagement with the present moment, fostering a deep connection to one's surroundings.

Historical practices of mindfulness and presence are particularly relevant in intentional living. Cultures worldwide have long recognized the power of cultivating awareness in daily activities. For instance, the Japanese concept of "ichi-go ichi-e" emphasizes the uniqueness of each moment and the importance of being fully present.

This philosophy encourages individuals to savor their experiences, fostering gratitude and appreciation for life's fleeting beauty. By understanding these historical contexts, modern practitioners can better appreciate the significance of stillness as a transformative practice that aligns with their values.

The intersection of Eastern philosophy and Western wellness has seen a resurgence of interest in the principles of non-action and stillness. As contemporary society becomes increasingly fast-paced and chaotic, many individuals turn to these ancient teachings for balance and clarity.

Historical figures like Laozi and Confucius laid the groundwork for a philosophy that values simplicity, humility, and understanding one's place within the cosmos. This historical relevance reminds us that the quest for meaning and balance is not a new endeavor but a timeless pursuit shared across cultures.

The modern movement toward digital detox and sustainable living reflects a growing awareness of the need for stillness in our lives. As technology permeates every aspect of existence, the historical understanding of stillness counterbalances the constant noise and distractions.

Individuals can cultivate a deeper connection to the natural world and their inner selves by disconnecting from digital stimuli and embracing moments of stillness. This historical perspective emphasizes that stepping back is not a retreat but a vital step toward reconnection and rejuvenation.

Ultimately, the historical context of stillness and non-action underscores its relevance in contemporary life. As individuals seek to harmonize their lifestyles with nature and personal values, the lessons from the past serve as guiding principles.

Embracing the philosophy of stillness allows for a more meaningful existence, encouraging a life that is not only aligned with individual aspirations but also deeply rooted in previous generations' wisdom. This timeless pursuit of balance through non-action empowers individuals to navigate the complexities of modern life with grace and resilience.

The Practice of Wuwei

In a world that constantly demands our attention and action, profound wisdom encourages us to do the opposite: to let go of our need for control and allow life to unfold naturally. This ancient philosophy, known as wuwei, or non-action, speaks to the power of presence and the art of effortless living. By embracing the principle of wuwei, we can discover a sense of freedom and acceptance often eluded in our fast-paced, achievement-driven lives.

At its core, wuwei is about aligning ourselves with the natural rhythms of the universe rather than trying to manipulate or dominate the world around us. It's about cultivating a sense of inner calm and clarity and allowing solutions to emerge organically rather than forcing them. This approach leads to more harmonious outcomes and fosters a more profound understanding of connection with ourselves, others, and the natural world.

In the following pages, we will delve into the practical applications of wuwei, exploring how this timeless wisdom can be integrated into our daily lives. We will examine how wuwei can help us cultivate greater awareness, acceptance, and inner peace and how it can inform our relationships, decision-making, and overall well-being.

By embracing the principle of wuwei, we can experience a profound shift in our perspective, allowing us to navigate life's challenges with greater ease, clarity, and wisdom.

As we embark on this journey of discovery, we will explore the intersections between wuwei and mindfulness and how these two practices can complement each other in powerful ways. We will also examine how wuwei can be applied in our personal and professional lives, from the simplest tasks to the most complex challenges. By the end of this exploration, we will have a deeper understanding of the transformative power of wuwei and how it can help us live a more authentic, fulfilling, and harmonious existence.

The Philosophy of Non-Action and Its Relevance Today

The philosophy of wuwei, or non-action, emphasizes the power of presence and letting things unfold naturally. By practicing non-action, we can learn to let go of the ego's need for control and find freedom in acceptance. Wuwei encourages a flow and effortless action rather than forced effort, which can lead to more harmonious outcomes.

In today's fast-paced world, wuwei counterbalances the constant pressure of productivity and achievement. Embracing non-action can help cultivate inner calm, reduce stress, and respond to life's challenges with greater clarity and wisdom. The principle of wuwei is deeply rooted in Taoist and Buddhist traditions, promoting the idea of aligning with the natural rhythms of the universe.

Applying the philosophy of wuwei in daily life can help us become more present, attuned to our surroundings, and responsive to the moment's needs. It encourages us to focus on being rather than doing, allowing solutions to emerge organically rather than forcing them.

Wuwei is not about passivity or inaction but rather about acting with a light touch and a sense of ease. In our personal and professional lives, we can practice mindfulness and meditation to cultivate a sense of inner calm and clarity.

We can also adopt a more flexible and adaptable approach to decision-making, allowing us to respond to changing circumstances with greater ease and wisdom. We can create more harmonious and mutually beneficial relationships by letting go of our need to control and dominate.

We can also adopt a more listening and receptive approach to understand better and respond to others' needs. This can lead to more effective communication and collaboration and a more profound connection and understanding with others.

By incorporating wuwei into our daily lives, we can experience various benefits, from reduced stress and anxiety to improved relationships and decision-making. It is a powerful tool for cultivating greater awareness, acceptance, and inner peace. As we continue to navigate the complexities of modern life, the wisdom of wuwei can provide a valuable guide and inspiration for living a more balanced, harmonious, and fulfilling existence.

The practice of wuwei requires patience, self-awareness, and a willingness to let go of our attachment to outcomes. This journey requires us to be gentle with ourselves and others and approach life's challenges with curiosity and openness. By embracing the principle of wuwei, we can tap into a more profound understanding of purpose and meaning and live a more authentic and fulfilling life.

Ultimately, the practice of wuwei is a reminder that life is not about achieving a specific outcome or goal but about being present in the moment and allowing things to unfold naturally. By embracing this approach, we can find greater peace, clarity, and wisdom and live in harmony with the natural world.

Letting Go of Control and Embracing Spontaneity

Letting go of control is a crucial and transformative step toward embracing spontaneity, ultimately leading to a more dynamic and fulfilling life. In a world often dominated by tightly packed schedules, societal expectations, and the relentless pressures of responsibility, the desire to maintain control can become overwhelming, leaving us feeling constrained and stifled.

This drive for control can create a rigid framework that restricts our creativity and diminishes life's opportunities for joy, exploration, and personal growth.
When we consciously choose to let go of our grip on control, we open ourselves to the unpredictable facets of life.

Embracing spontaneity invites a refreshing sense of playfulness and adventure, allowing us to engage with our surroundings and the people within them. This shift in mindset fosters more profound connections with ourselves and others in ways we may not have anticipated, expanding our horizons and enriching our everyday experiences.

It's important to clarify that embracing spontaneity doesn't equate to being reckless or abandoning all responsibility. Instead, it involves cultivating a mindset that welcomes flexibility, adaptability, and luck.

This approach encourages us to tune into our instincts and desires in the moment, facilitating a more profound and more vibrant experience of life. For example, whether it's taking an impromptu trip to a nearby town, experimenting with a new hobby that catches our interest, or simply saying yes to an unplanned invitation from a friend, these small acts of spontaneity can awaken a profound sense of freedom and creativity within us.

By letting go of the illusion of control, we enrich our lives and discover the beauty in allowing life to unfold naturally. This mindset invites a more profound sense of authenticity and presence into our daily experiences, helping us appreciate the journey rather than fixating solely on the destination.

This shift encourages us to savor each moment and embrace life's richness, reminding us that the most meaningful experiences sometimes arise from the unpredictability we often seek to avoid.

The Connection Between Wuwei and Mindfulness

Wuwei, a concept deeply rooted in Daoist philosophy, is frequently translated as "non-action" or "effortless action." However, this translation needs to be more accurate, as Wuwei is more about aligning oneself with the natural flow of life than about actual inaction.

It encourages individuals to move harmoniously with the universe's rhythms rather than resist or struggle against them. This approach fosters a sense of fluidity and adaptability, allowing life to unfold organically.

This idea resonates closely with the principles of mindfulness, which emphasizes a deep presence and engagement in the current moment without the imposition of judgments or distractions.

Both practices invite individuals to let go of the constant desire for control—an urge that often leads to stress and frustration. Instead, they advocate cultivating a heightened awareness that empowers us to respond to life's challenges gracefully and effortlessly. By incorporating Wuwei into one's life, one can cultivate mindfulness, experiencing acceptance and tranquility.

This perspective acknowledges that there are times when the most effective course of action is not to strive for specific outcomes but to embrace existence as it is simply. Moreover, the connection between Wuwei and mindfulness deepens our understanding of balance in an increasingly fast-paced world.

Many people find themselves caught in a cycle of relentless productivity, where the pressure to achieve and perform can overshadow their well-being. Both Wuwei and mindfulness serve as gentle reminders of the significance of pausing—of tuning into ourselves and our environment. Integrating moments of stillness and reflection into our daily routines allows us to cultivate inner peace that transcends chaos.

This practice enhances self-awareness and enriches our interactions with others and the world. Embracing Wuwei allows individuals to take a mindful approach to life, where spontaneity and intuition lead the way. It encourages letting go of rigid plans and expectations and instead trusting in the process of life.

This shift in perspective can result in a more harmonious existence, where we flow with circumstances rather than fighting against them. By fostering this balance between action and inaction, we find ourselves better equipped to navigate life's challenges, nurturing a state of grace that permeates our thoughts, actions, and relationships.

Applying non-action in Everyday Life

Embracing the concept of non-action in our everyday lives is intricately linked with the philosophy of wuwei, a principle deeply rooted in Taoist thought. Wuwei emphasizes the importance of flowing through life's routines with a sense of tranquility and naturalness, as opposed to the relentless pursuit of effort and control that often defines our modern existence.

This philosophy invites us to consciously disengage from the ceaseless race for achievement, encouraging moments of stillness, introspection, and mindfulness. In practice, this approach transforms how we engage with our daily tasks. For example, we can embrace the present moment more fully rather than rushing through our responsibilities with a fixed mindset focused solely on checking items off a to-do list.
This might involve pausing to take a deep breath when we feel overwhelmed, allowing ourselves to observe our thoughts and emotions without judgment, and responding to life's challenges with a sense of awareness rather than reflexivity.

Such a non-reactive approach can significantly enhance our decision-making abilities, enabling us to respond thoughtfully and creatively to life's unpredictability while cultivating a more profound inner calm.

In concrete terms, applying the principle of non-action can take many forms in our daily lives. It could involve practicing mindfulness during simple, everyday activities. For instance, while enjoying a meal, instead of becoming distracted by technology or multitasking, we might fully immerse ourselves in the experience—appreciating our food's flavors, textures, and aromas. Or, during a walk, we can strive to become attuned to the sights, sounds, and sensations around us, allowing us to engage with nature and our environment truly.

By relinquishing the constant need to control every facet of our lives, we create space for spontaneity and inspiration. This shift alleviates stress and anxiety and enriches our connection to the present moment. Engaging with life this way fosters a more genuine connection with ourselves and the world around us, allowing us to experience life more profoundly.

Ultimately, integrating non-action into our daily routines can facilitate a significant transformation. It helps us balance doing and being, leading to a more harmonious existence. By navigating the complexities of modern life with an open heart and mind, we can cultivate a lasting sense of peace and tranquility that enhances our overall well-being, allowing us to thrive amid the busyness that characterizes contemporary living.

The Liberating Power of Non-Action in a Busy World

In our fast-paced world, where productivity is often equated with self-worth, the concept of non-action may seem paradoxical. However, the liberating power of non-action offers a refreshing perspective that encourages us to step back, breathe, and reassess our approach to daily life.

Embracing non-action isn't about doing nothing but creating a space for introspection. This allows us to tune into our true selves and foster authentic connections with our surroundings. When we adopt a mindset of non-action, we liberate ourselves from the constant pressure to perform, enabling our minds to clear and our creativity to flourish.

In many ways, non-action is a radical counterbalance to the relentless pursuit of achievement that defines modern existence. By resisting the urge to overcommit and overexert ourselves, we can cultivate awareness and presence that clarifies our intentions and decisions.

This practice teaches us to discern between what requires our energy and attention and what may simply be a distraction. In moments of stillness, we find space to listen—both to ourselves and the environment around us—leading to deeper insights and a more meaningful way of engaging with life.

Moreover, embracing non-action empowers us to let go of control, allowing life to unfold in its own time. In doing so, we embrace spontaneity and open ourselves to unexpected opportunities we may have overlooked.

By stepping back from the relentless drive for accomplishment, we allow ourselves to be guided by our intrinsic rhythms and the natural flow of life. Ultimately, we find greater joy in the journey rather than fixating solely on the destination. In this liberating practice, we reclaim the essence of living fully and authentically, where peace resides in the profound simplicity of simply being.

Chapter 6

Digital Detox

The Need for Digital Disconnect

The pervasive presence of digital technology in our lives has transformed the way we interact with the world around us. While these advancements offer convenience and connectivity, they create a barrier to genuine engagement with our surroundings.

The need for a digital disconnect arises from the recognition that constant access to screens and notifications often detracts from our ability to experience the richness of the present moment. By removing digital distractions, we create space for deeper connections with nature, ourselves, and those we cherish.

Nature immersion is a profound antidote to the digital noise surrounding us. When we immerse ourselves in the natural world, we are invited to engage our senses fully, noticing the intricate details of our environment—the rustle of leaves, the scent of pine, and the vibrant hues of a sunset.

These experiences cultivate presence, allowing us to reconnect with our innate rhythms and life cycles. In contrast, the digital world often presents a curated and filtered reality, leading to disconnection from nature's genuine experiences. By prioritizing outdoor experiences over screen time, we foster a sense of belonging within the natural ecosystem.

Intentional living emphasizes aligning our daily choices with our core values. In a society that often equates success with constant connectivity and productivity, the practice of digital disconnect invites us to reevaluate our priorities.

By consciously choosing when and how we engage with technology, we reclaim our time and focus on what truly matters. This intentional approach allows us to design a life that reflects our values, whether dedicating time to family, pursuing hobbies, or simply enjoying solitude in nature. Unplugging can be a powerful statement of our commitment to living authentically and mindfully.

The philosophy of non-action, or wuwei, offers an essential perspective on the necessity of stepping back from our digital devices. Wuwei teaches us the value of effortless action and allowing things to unfold naturally. In a world that often promotes a culture of busyness and constant achievement, embracing stillness can lead to greater clarity and insight.

By disconnecting from digital demands, we open ourselves up to moments of reflection and creativity that the constant buzz of notifications would otherwise drown out. This mindful approach encourages us to trust in life, allowing things to happen independently.

Finally, gratitude, primarily through the lens of amor fati, or love of fate, becomes more accessible when we disconnect from digital distractions. Engaging fully with the present allows us to appreciate the beauty and complexity of our experiences, even the challenging ones.

By stepping away from screens, we create opportunities to reflect on our lives and cultivate a sense of acceptance for our circumstances. This deepened gratitude enhances our well-being and reinforces our connection to nature and the community. The digital disconnect is not merely a retreat from technology but an invitation to embrace a more meaningful and balanced way of living.

The Impact of Technology on Our Mental and Physical Health

The relentless integration of technology into our daily lives has far-reaching consequences on our well-being, contributing to heightened anxiety, depression, and cognitive decline. Constant digital stimulation disrupts our natural sleep cycles, leading to fatigue, reduced productivity, and impaired physical health. The perpetual need to be "always on" and the pressure to respond instantly to notifications can induce chronic stress and burnout.

Moreover, the addictive nature of specific digital platforms and apps can foster compulsive behaviors, disrupting work-life balance and interpersonal connections. The lack of face-to-face interactions and physical touch due to digital interactions can negatively impact our emotional and social development. For instance, studies have shown that children who spend more time on screens tend to have lower social skills and increased rates of depression.

The consequences of excessive technology use can be devastating. When we're constantly connected, we can feel isolated, even amid crowds. We may become detached from our surroundings, unable to engage with the world around us fully. Our minds become consumed by the never-ending stream of information, leaving us feeling overwhelmed and anxious.

It's essential to recognize technology's impact on our lives and take steps to mitigate its harmful effects. This can be achieved by setting boundaries, such as designing screen-free zones and times and engaging in activities promoting face-to-face interaction. By being mindful of our technology use and making conscious choices, we can reduce the risk of developing mental health issues and improve our overall well-being.

There has been a growing awareness of the need for balance in recent years. People are beginning to recognize the importance of disconnecting from technology and reconnecting with the world around them. By taking a step back and reassessing our relationship with technology, we can create a healthier, more balanced lifestyle that promotes mental and emotional well-being.

As we navigate the complexities of modern life, it's crucial to prioritize our mental health and well-being. By being aware of the potential risks of excessive technology use and taking steps to mitigate them, we can create a more sustainable and balanced lifestyle that promotes overall well-being.

Excessive technology use can also lead to feelings of loneliness and disconnection. We may find ourselves substituting online interactions for in-person connections, leading to isolation and disconnection from others. Furthermore, the constant stream of information can be overwhelming, making it difficult to focus and be present in the moment.

By taking control of our technology use and making conscious choices, we can reduce the adverse effects of excessive technology use and promote a healthier, more balanced lifestyle. This can be achieved by setting boundaries, engaging in activities that promote face-to-face interaction, and being mindful of our technology use. Doing so can improve our mental and emotional well-being and create a more sustainable and balanced lifestyle.

Ultimately, it's up to each individual to take responsibility for technology use and make conscious choices to promote a healthier relationship with technology. By being aware of the potential risks and taking steps to mitigate them, we can create a more balanced and sustainable lifestyle that promotes overall well-being.

Strategies for a Meaningful Digital Detox

A digital detox has become vital for cultivating presence and awareness in an age of constant connectivity. One effective strategy for a meaningful digital detox is to establish clear boundaries around technology use. This involves setting specific times for checking emails and social media, allowing for uninterrupted periods of focus on personal values and activities that resonate with one's true self.

By intentionally segmenting your day, you create a structured environment where technology does not overshadow your interactions with nature or the practices that enhance your well-being.

Another powerful approach is to engage in nature immersion. Spending time outdoors can significantly counterbalance the effects of digital overexposure. Whether through hiking, gardening, or simply sitting in a park, immersing oneself in natural surroundings fosters a deeper connection to the present moment.

This reduces the temptation to reach for digital devices and enhances physical and mental health. Prioritizing nature as a refuge allows individuals to recharge and reflect, reinforcing the philosophy of non-action by promoting stillness and observation over constant engagement.

Incorporating intentional living into your digital detox can further deepen your experience. This means aligning your daily habits and choices with your core values, which can be achieved through mindful practices like journaling or meditation.

Reflecting on what truly matters to you helps clarify which digital interactions support your life purpose and which detract from it. By consciously choosing to engage with technology that enriches your life—such as educational podcasts or virtual community gatherings—you can ensure that your digital consumption becomes a tool for growth rather than a source of distraction.

Gratitude practices also play a significant role in this detox journey. Cultivating a mindset of acceptance through techniques such as amor fati—loving your fate—encourages individuals to appreciate their current circumstances, including their relationship with technology.

One can foster a balanced perspective by recognizing the benefits and lessons learned from both digital tools and their absence. Developing a daily gratitude ritual can help shift one's focus from what one lacks in one's digital life to the richness of present experiences, enhancing one's overall outlook.

Finally, embracing sustainable living principles can provide a holistic framework for your digital detox. By harmonizing lifestyle choices with nature, you reinforce the importance of making intentional decisions in all aspects of life.

This includes reducing reliance on technology that disrupts harmony and choosing alternatives that promote well-being and environmental consciousness. Adopting sustainable practices enriches your connection to the earth and reminds you that a slower, more meaningful life is attainable through mindful choices, both digital and otherwise.

In today's digital age, cultivating a healthy relationship with technology is essential for mental and emotional well-being. It begins with setting boundaries on screen time to ensure that technology enhances rather than hinders our daily lives.

Establishing specific times for device use, especially during meals or before bedtime, can foster more meaningful interactions with family and friends. Additionally, being intentional about our content is crucial; choosing educational and uplifting materials can positively influence our mood and mindset.

Furthermore, taking regular breaks from technology is vital for mental rejuvenation. Engaging in outdoor exercise, reading physical books, or practicing mindfulness offers a balanced approach that reduces screen dependency.

By cultivating awareness of how technology impacts our lives and focusing on quality interactions, we can create a healthier, more fulfilling relationship with the digital world, ensuring it serves as a tool for connectivity rather than a source of distraction.

Creating a Healthy Relationship with Technology

Creating a healthy relationship with technology requires a conscious effort rooted in intentionality and self-awareness. In our current landscape, where screens dominate personal and professional interactions, it becomes crucial to establish clear boundaries that prioritize our well-being.

This process starts with setting aside designated times for engaging with media and technology. By doing so, we can ensure that using these tools enhances our lives rather than becoming a constant source of distraction.

Implementing regular digital detoxes can also play a significant role in fostering this healthy relationship. Taking breaks from screens allows us to step back from the digital world and reconnect with our immediate environment. These breaks encourage us to engage in meaningful face-to-face conversations, enjoy nature, or reflect on our thoughts. By experiencing life without the filter of a screen, we open ourselves up to more prosperous, more authentic interactions and personal reflections.

Moreover, cultivating mindfulness during technological engagements can significantly enhance the overall experience. Mindfulness in this context means being fully present during digital interactions, whether via video call with a friend or a simple scroll through social media.

It involves intentionally selecting content that contributes positively to our lives—educational videos, inspirational articles, or uplifting music—while actively managing notifications to minimize unnecessary interruptions.

Incorporating reflective practices into our technology use can also promote a balanced approach. This might involve pausing to evaluate how specific applications, platforms, or online content make us feel. Are they inspiring, uplifting, or educational, or do they lead to feelings of anxiety, inadequacy, or distraction? By becoming more aware of our emotional responses to technology, we can make more informed choices about how we engage with it.

Ultimately, nurturing a balanced relationship with technology enables us to harness its myriad benefits, such as improved communication and access to information, and safeguards our mental and emotional health.

By intentionally managing our interactions with technology, we empower ourselves to create a fulfilling and enriching experience that aligns with our values and supports our overall well-being.

Reconnecting with the Present Moment

In today's digital age, a healthy relationship with technology is essential for maintaining our well-being and fostering meaningful connections. It begins with self-awareness; recognizing how technology influences our daily lives—both positively and negatively—is crucial.

Setting boundaries around device usage can help mitigate feelings of overwhelm, allowing us to reclaim valuable time for ourselves and our relationships. This might mean designating tech-free zones in our homes, scheduling regular breaks from screens, or adopting "digital detox" practices to refresh our mental state.

Moreover, being intentional about the technology we engage with can enhance our experiences. Seeking platforms that promote genuine interaction and learning rather than mindless consumption can lead to deeper connections and a more enriching online presence.

Emphasizing quality over quantity in our digital interactions can significantly improve our mental health, fostering a sense of presence and connection in a world that often encourages distraction.

By cultivating mindfulness around our technology use, we can ensure it becomes a tool for growth, connection, and creativity rather than a source of stress or disconnection. Reconnecting with the present moment is essential in our fast-paced, digitally-driven world.

Many individuals find themselves caught in a relentless cycle of distraction, where the past influences their thoughts, and the future creates anxiety. This disconnect can impede our ability to engage with life fully and appreciate our experiences' richness.

By cultivating a practice of stillness, we can learn to immerse ourselves in the present. This allows us to notice the subtleties of our surroundings and foster a deeper connection with ourselves and nature.

Nature immersion is a powerful tool in this journey of reconnection. Spending time outdoors rejuvenates the spirit and anchors us here and now. The sights and sounds of nature—rustling leaves, flowing water, or the call of birds—offer a sensory experience that brings our awareness back to the present.

Engaging with these elements encourages mindfulness, helping us to observe our thoughts and feelings without judgment. This practice can bridge the gap between our inner lives and the external world, reinforcing our sense of belonging and balance.

Intentional living further supports the process of reconnecting with the present moment. We create an authentic and fulfilling life by aligning our daily activities with our core values. Each choice becomes an opportunity to practice presence, whether savoring a meal, enjoying a conversation, or simply taking a moment to breathe.

This alignment fosters gratitude for the current moment, allowing us to appreciate what we have rather than focusing on what we lack. When our actions reflect our values, we cultivate a more profound sense of contentment in our daily lives.

The philosophy of non-action, or wuwei, invites us to embrace a state of flow rather than striving forcefully for outcomes. This approach teaches us that by letting go of the need to control every aspect of our lives, we can find a natural rhythm that aligns with the present moment.

In a society that often equates busyness with productivity, wuwei offers a refreshing perspective, encouraging us to pause, reflect, and allow life to unfold. This practice can lead to profound insights and a clearer understanding of our purpose, enhancing our ability to live in the now.

Finally, integrating gratitude practices into our daily routine can further deepen our connection to the present. Embracing the philosophy of amor fati—loving one's fate—encourages acceptance of life's circumstances, promoting resilience and peace of mind.

By expressing gratitude for the challenges and the joys we encounter, we cultivate a mindset that recognizes the beauty in every moment. This attitude enhances our well-being and strengthens our ties to the world around us, fostering a sustainable lifestyle that honors our journeys and the interconnectedness of all living things.

Chapter 7

Sustainable Living

Principles of Sustainable Lifestyle Choices

Sustainable lifestyle choices are grounded in principles that promote harmony between individual needs and the planet's well-being. Central to these choices is the understanding that every action has a ripple effect.

By consciously selecting how we live, consume, and interact with our environment, we can cultivate a lifestyle that enriches our lives and contributes positively to the ecosystem. The essence of sustainable living lies in recognizing our interconnectedness with nature and choosing practices that support ecological balance, resource conservation, and biodiversity.

The principle of intentional living serves as a foundation for sustainable choices. This involves aligning daily activities with personal values, often including a commitment to environmental stewardship. Individuals can engage in practices such as mindful consumption, where the emphasis is placed on purchasing local, organic, and ethically sourced products.

This reduces carbon footprints and fosters community and support for regional economies. By making deliberate choices reflecting personal values, individuals contribute to a more significant movement toward sustainability, demonstrating that lifestyle changes can be meaningful and impactful.

Another key principle involves the philosophy of non-action or Wuwei, which advocates for an approach to life that emphasizes ease and natural flow. Sustainable living can mean simplifying one's lifestyle by reducing excess and embracing minimalism.

By letting go of unnecessary possessions and distractions, individuals create space for a more intentional existence that prioritizes quality over quantity. This principle encourages a deeper connection to nature, as spending time outdoors fosters a sense of presence and appreciation for the world around us, reinforcing the importance of protecting it.

Gratitude practices play a significant role in fostering a sustainable lifestyle. By cultivating an attitude of appreciation for what we have, individuals can shift their focus from consumerism to contentment.

This practice aligns with the concept of Amor Fati, or love of fate, which encourages acceptance of life's circumstances and a recognition of the beauty inherent in simplicity. When individuals express gratitude for the natural resources that sustain us, they are more likely to adopt behaviors that protect and preserve those resources, leading to a more sustainable existence.

Finally, the concept of a digital detox is essential in the quest for a sustainable lifestyle. In a world increasingly dominated by technology, disengaging from screens allows individuals to reconnect with their surroundings and engage more fully with nature. This disconnection fosters mindfulness and presence, enabling an appreciation for the environment that can often be overlooked in the hustle of modern life. By prioritizing time spent outdoors and embracing stillness, individuals can cultivate a deeper understanding of their place in the ecosystem, encouraging lifestyle choices that honor personal well-being and the planet's health.

Harmonizing Daily Life with Nature

Harmonizing daily life with nature involves recognizing the interconnectedness between our rhythms and the natural world. This alignment may seem elusive in a society dominated by technology and constant stimulation. Yet, cultivating a lifestyle prioritizing natural experiences can foster a profound sense of presence and peace. Engaging with nature encourages mindfulness and reinforces our values, enabling us to live more intentionally. This process facilitates a deeper understanding of ourselves and our place within the larger ecosystem.

To truly harmonize with nature, one must first cultivate awareness of its cycles and rhythms. Observing the changing seasons, the patterns of wildlife, and the subtle shifts in weather can provide valuable insights into the flow of life.

Integrating these observations into our daily routines can help us embrace a more organic lifestyle. This might mean adjusting our schedules to align with daylight hours, incorporating outdoor activities throughout the week, or planning meals around seasonal produce. Such practices enhance our connection to nature and promote sustainability by minimizing our ecological footprint.

The philosophy of non-action, or wuwei, offers a framework for harmonizing our lives with the natural world. Wuwei emphasizes effortless action, aligning our intentions with the natural flow of life rather than forcing outcomes. Practicing wuwei teaches us to trust the process and allow nature to guide us.

This approach can manifest in various ways, such as adopting a more flexible mindset regarding our goals, engaging in spontaneous outdoor activities, or allowing our creative expressions to emerge without undue pressure. Embracing this philosophy can lead to a more authentic existence rooted in the present moment.

Gratitude practices play a significant role in harmonizing daily life with nature, fostering a sense of acceptance and appreciation for the world around us. By cultivating gratitude, we can shift our focus from what we lack to the abundance in our natural surroundings.

Simple practices, such as keeping a gratitude journal or taking time each day to acknowledge the beauty of the environment, can deepen our connection to nature and enhance our overall well-being. This acceptance, aligned with the concept of amor fati, encourages us to embrace life as it unfolds, recognizing that every experience contributes to our growth.

In a digital age marked by constant connectivity, a digital detox can serve as a crucial step toward harmonizing our lives with nature.

Disconnecting from screens and technology allows us to engage more fully with the natural world and our immediate surroundings.

This intentional break can increase mindfulness, improve relationships, and increase appreciation for life's simple pleasures. By prioritizing outdoor experiences and fostering meaningful connections with nature and others, we can create a life that reflects our values and nurtures our well-being, ultimately leading to a more balanced and fulfilling existence.

Building a Community of Sustainability

Building a community of sustainability is not merely a collective effort toward ecological preservation; it embodies a holistic approach to living that harmonizes individual values with shared goals. In the modern world, where rapid consumption often overshadows mindful living, creating a sustainable community involves cultivating a space where individuals feel empowered to align their lifestyles with the rhythms of nature. This requires fostering an environment that encourages dialogue, education, and mutual support among community members who share a commitment to intentional living.

At the heart of this community lies the philosophy of non-action, or wuwei, which teaches that the most effective way to engage with the world is through a gentle approach that respects the natural order. Embracing this principle allows individuals to recognize their place within the larger ecosystem and encourages them to take thoughtful and impactful action.

Community members can better understand their roles in promoting sustainability by prioritizing stillness and reflection. This can lead to actions that resonate with their core values rather than ones driven by external pressures.

Nature immersion is pivotal in cultivating presence and awareness, which are essential to a sustainable community. By engaging with the natural world, individuals can experience firsthand the interconnectedness of all living things.

Outdoor experiences become a source of inspiration and motivation, reminding community members of the beauty and fragility of their environment. This connection fosters a sense of responsibility and stewardship, encouraging individuals to advocate for practices that enhance ecological balance and promote sustainable living.

Gratitude practices contribute significantly to the foundation of a sustainability-oriented community. By cultivating an attitude of acceptance and appreciation for what nature provides, individuals can shift their focus from a scarcity mindset to one of abundance.

Embracing the concept of amor fati, or love of fate, further deepens this appreciation, allowing community members to find joy and purpose even in challenges related to environmental issues. This perspective nurtures resilience and encourages individuals to remain committed to sustainable practices, understanding that each action contributes to a more significant positive impact, no matter how small.

Finally, a digital detox is essential for fostering genuine connections within the community. In a world saturated with distractions and constant connectivity, disconnecting allows individuals to engage more fully with their surroundings and each other. This slower pace of life creates opportunities for meaningful conversations and shared experiences that strengthen community bonds.

Members cultivate a supportive environment reinforcing their commitment to sustainability and intentional living by prioritizing face-to-face interactions and immersing themselves in the natural world. This ultimately creates a vibrant community aligned with their shared values.

Chapter 8

Eastern Philosophy Meets Western Wellness

Bridging Philosophical Traditions

Bridging philosophical traditions can be a powerful tool for independent-minded individuals seeking a more intentional life in the quest for balance through non-action. Eastern philosophies, particularly those rooted in Taoism, emphasize the concept of wuwei, or non-action, which encourages individuals to align themselves with the natural flow of life rather than resist it.

This principle resonates deeply with nature immersion, where spending time in natural environments fosters a sense of presence and awareness. By integrating the wisdom of wuwei with Western approaches to wellness, individuals can cultivate a lifestyle that is reflective and responsive to the rhythms of the world around them.

Intentional living, a core focus for many independent thinkers, often draws from diverse philosophical traditions to craft a life that aligns with personal values. The principles of wuwei can complement modern notions of minimalism and simplicity, advocating for a life unencumbered by excess and distraction.

By embracing the idea of non-action, individuals can prioritize their values more effectively, allowing for a more genuine expression of self. This integration of Eastern and Western thought enriches the philosophy of intentional living and promotes a deeper understanding of navigating life's complexities with grace and ease.

In gratitude practices, the concept of amor fati, or love of fate, emerges as a pivotal element that harmonizes well with Eastern and Western philosophical traditions. Embracing what life presents rather than resisting it aligns closely with the principles of wuwei, fostering acceptance and resilience.

This approach encourages individuals to cultivate a mindset of appreciation for their experiences, leading to a more profound connection with themselves and their surroundings. By bridging these traditions, individuals can develop practices that enhance their ability to find joy and meaning, regardless of life's challenges.

Digital detox strategies also benefit from the synthesis of these philosophical perspectives. In a world dominated by technology, disconnection becomes paramount for those seeking a slower, more meaningful life.

The teachings of wuwei advocate for a harmonious relationship with one's environment, suggesting that constant engagement with digital devices can disrupt this balance. By applying principles from both Eastern and Western philosophies, individuals can create intentional digital boundaries that promote mindfulness and presence, allowing them to reconnect with the natural world and their inner selves.

Finally, sustainable living emerges as a critical intersection where these philosophical traditions coalesce. The commitment to harmonizing lifestyle choices with nature is deeply embedded in Eastern thought, which often emphasizes living following natural laws and contemporary Western practices aimed at environmental stewardship.

By bridging these traditions, individuals can cultivate a lifestyle that respects the planet and embodies the essence of non-action. This approach encourages a thoughtful engagement with consumption, urging independence from societal pressures that advocate for constant growth and accumulation. By embracing a philosophy that values stillness and presence, individuals can contribute to a more sustainable and meaningful existence, ultimately enhancing their connection to nature and themselves.

Integrating Eastern Practices into Modern Life

Integrating Eastern practices into modern life involves a thoughtful approach that bridges ancient wisdom with contemporary experiences. At the core of this integration lies the philosophy of non-action, or

Wuwei, which emphasizes the importance of aligning with the natural flow of life rather than forcing outcomes.

By embracing this principle, individuals can cultivate a sense of ease and presence in their daily activities. This mindset encourages a deeper awareness of one's surroundings, fostering a connection with nature that enhances mental and physical well-being.

Nature immersion serves as a practical context for applying Eastern philosophies. Engaging with the natural world allows individuals to step away from the chaos of modern life and reconnect with their inner selves.

Activities such as hiking, gardening, or simply sitting in a park can evoke a state of mindfulness, where one becomes attuned to the rhythms of nature. This immersion fosters presence and reinforces gratitude for life's simple joys, aligning perfectly with the principles of intentional living.

By designing a life that prioritizes time in nature, individuals can cultivate a deeper appreciation for their environment and the interconnectedness of all living things.

Gratitude further enriches intentional living, mainly through the lens of Amor Fati. This philosophy advocates embracing one's fate with acceptance and love and encourages individuals to recognize the beauty in every experience, even those that may seem challenging.

By integrating gratitude practices into daily routines, such as journaling or mindful reflection, individuals can shift their perspectives and find meaning in their circumstances. This enhances personal values and promotes a balanced approach to life, fostering resilience and adaptability in adversity.

A digital detox is another essential component of integrating Eastern practices into modern life. The constant barrage of information and connectivity can lead to a sense of overwhelm, detracting from the stillness and presence that Eastern philosophies advocate. Individuals can intentionally disconnect from digital distractions to create space for reflection and self-discovery.

This practice aligns with the philosophy of non-action, allowing individuals to observe their thoughts and feelings without the noise of external stimuli. The result is a more meaningful and purposeful existence, where decisions are made from a place of clarity rather than reaction.

Finally, sustainable living plays a crucial role in harmonizing lifestyle choices with nature, an integral aspect of Eastern practices. By adopting environmentally conscious habits, individuals can live in alignment with their values while fostering a sense of community and responsibility toward the Earth.

This includes mindful consumption, supporting local economies, and engaging in practices that nurture the planet. Through this integration, individuals contribute to the well-being of their environment and experience a profound sense of purpose and fulfillment in their lives, ultimately embodying the principles of balance and harmony that Eastern philosophies promote.

The Role of Stillness in Holistic Health

Stillness plays a pivotal role in holistic health by fostering a deeper connection between mind, body, and spirit. In a world that often glorifies busyness and constant activity, embracing stillness can seem counterintuitive.

However, individuals can be more aware of their internal landscapes through quiet reflection and intentional pauses. This awareness enables a more profound understanding of one's needs, desires, and values, leading to a more aligned lifestyle with holistic health principles.

Engaging with nature is a powerful way to harness the benefits of stillness. Immersing oneself in natural surroundings allows for a unique opportunity to disconnect from the frenetic pace of modern life. Nature's inherent tranquility encourages individuals to slow down, breathe deeply, and observe the world around them.

This immersion enhances presence and nurtures a sense of belonging to something larger than oneself, essential for emotional and spiritual well-being. The stillness found in nature can catalyze introspection, promoting clarity and a more centered approach to daily challenges.

Intentional living is intricately linked to the practice of stillness. By incorporating quiet moments into daily routines, individuals can create space for reflection and evaluation of their life choices.

This practice of non-action encourages a more thoughtful approach to decision-making, allowing for alignment with personal values and goals. When stillness is embraced, it becomes easier to discern what truly matters, fostering a sense of purpose and fulfillment. As one steps back from the chaos of everyday life, the clarity gained from stillness can lead to more meaningful and sustainable choices.

The philosophy of non-action, or Wuwei, emphasizes the importance of effortless action and alignment with the natural flow of life. In a holistic health context, this principle encourages individuals to let go of the need to control every aspect of their lives.

Practicing stillness can cultivate a sense of acceptance and trust in life. This acceptance is essential for fostering resilience and adaptability when facing challenges. Integrating Wuwei into daily life allows for a more harmonious existence, where individuals can respond to situations with grace rather than force.

Finally, the intersection of Eastern philosophy and Western wellness practices highlights the significance of stillness in achieving overall health. Techniques such as mindfulness meditation, yoga, and deep breathing exercises draw on principles of stillness to promote mental clarity and emotional balance.

By incorporating these practices into daily routines, individuals can experience the profound benefits of slowing down. This digital detox from the constant stimulation of technology further enhances the ability to cultivate stillness, enabling a more meaningful engagement with life. Ultimately, embracing stillness as a core component of holistic health enhances personal well-being and fosters a deeper connection to the world around us.

Chapter 9

Cultivating a Practice of Stillness

Techniques for Daily Stillness

Various techniques can be used to cultivate daily stillness, encouraging individuals to pause, reflect, and connect with their inner selves. One effective method is mindfulness meditation, which focuses on the present moment.

This practice can be as simple as observing one's breath or the sounds of nature, allowing thoughts to come and go without attachment. By dedicating just a few minutes each day to mindfulness, individuals can create a space for stillness amidst the chaos of modern life.

This technique enhances awareness and fosters a deeper connection to the natural world, aligning perfectly with the principles of nature immersion.

Another valuable technique for achieving daily stillness is intentional living. This involves making conscious choices that reflect one's values and priorities. By identifying what truly matters, individuals can eliminate distractions and activities that do not serve their purpose.

Regularly assessing life goals and aligning daily actions with these intentions can create a sense of harmony and balance. Engaging in activities that resonate with one's values, such as volunteering in the community or spending time in nature, reinforces the commitment to a life of meaning and stillness.

Incorporating elements of the philosophy of non-action, or wuwei, can also enhance daily stillness. Wuwei encourages individuals to act per the natural flow of life rather than forcing outcomes.

This approach can be practiced by allowing situations to unfold organically, trusting the process, and responding thoughtfully rather than reactively. By embracing wuwei, one can experience a profound sense of peace and stillness, reducing the mental clutter often accompanying a fast-paced lifestyle. This technique invites a form of acceptance that aligns beautifully with the concept of amor fati, or love of fate, encouraging gratitude for life's circumstances.

Digital detox is another essential practice for fostering daily stillness. In our hyper-connected world, constant notifications and digital distractions can fragment attention and create a sense of urgency.

Setting aside specific times to unplug from devices can help individuals reconnect with themselves and their surroundings. Engaging in activities such as reading, journaling, or taking walks in nature during these digital-free moments promotes clarity and presence. By consciously disconnecting, individuals can cultivate an environment conducive to stillness and reflection.

Lastly, sustainable living practices can contribute significantly to daily stillness. Adopting a lifestyle that harmonizes with nature encourages a slower pace of life, allowing for moments of contemplation and gratitude.

Simple actions, such as growing a garden, participating in local conservation efforts, or reducing waste, can deepen one's appreciation for the environment and foster a sense of connectedness.

Integrating sustainable practices into daily routines enhances personal well-being and nurtures a broader sense of stillness within the community and the natural world. By embracing these techniques, individuals can experience the transformative power of stillness.

Creating a Personal Sanctuary

Creating a personal sanctuary is essential in cultivating stillness and balance. A refuge is not merely a physical space but also an emotional and mental haven where one can retreat from the chaos of modern existence.

To create this sanctuary, one must first identify the elements that resonate with their values and foster a deep sense of peace. This process begins with introspection, understanding what truly brings joy and tranquility. By recognizing these elements, individuals can design a space—indoors or outdoors—that reflects their inner selves, constantly reminding them of their commitment to intentional living.

In the context of nature immersion, creating a personal sanctuary often involves integrating natural elements into one's space. Nature has an inherent ability to ground us and restore our sense of presence.

Incorporating plants, natural light, and organic materials into your sanctuary can enhance the connection to the earth. This interaction with nature encourages mindfulness and can transform a simple area into a vibrant refuge that promotes relaxation and reflection.

Outdoor sanctuaries, such as gardens or quiet nooks in a park, are powerful reminders of nature's beauty and serenity. They allow for moments of stillness amidst the hustle and bustle of daily life.

As individuals strive for intentional living, curating their sanctuary in alignment with their values becomes crucial. This may involve decluttering physical spaces to eliminate distractions and create an atmosphere conducive to focus and peace.

It is essential to surround oneself with objects and symbols that resonate with one's beliefs and aspirations. Whether through art, books, or personal mementos, each item should serve as a reminder of the life one seeks to lead.

Individuals can create an environment that inspires and reinforces their commitment to living authentically by intentionally selecting these elements.

Incorporating the philosophy of non-action, or wuwei, into the design of a personal sanctuary invites a sense of ease and acceptance. Wuwei encourages us to embrace simplicity and let go of the need for constant activity.

A sanctuary designed around this principle can be a space that invites stillness rather than demands productivity. By including areas for meditation, quiet reading, or simply observing the world, this sanctuary becomes a place where one can practice the art of non-action, allowing thoughts to settle and clarity to emerge. The refuge serves as a physical space and a philosophy of life that champions balance and reflection.

Finally, gratitude practices can enhance the experience of a personal sanctuary, fostering a more profound sense of acceptance and appreciation for one's surroundings.

By cultivating gratitude, individuals can transform their sanctuary into a space of abundance where every element is cherished. Regularly acknowledging the beauty and tranquility within this space reinforces positive associations and encourages a mindset of contentment.

As one engages with their sanctuary through the lens of gratitude, it becomes a powerful tool for fostering harmony within oneself, aligning with the principles of sustainable living and the intersection of Eastern and Western wellness practices.

In this way, creating a personal sanctuary transcends mere aesthetics, becoming a profound expression of one's journey toward balance and fulfillment.

The Long-Term Benefits of Stillness

The practice of stillness offers profound long-term benefits that resonate deeply with the independent-minded individual seeking a harmonious life.

In a world that often glorifies constant activity and productivity, embracing non-action moments can enhance clarity of thought and emotional resilience. This clarity allows individuals to align more closely with their values, fostering a deeper understanding of their goals and the paths that lead to them.

By stepping back from the constant noise of daily life, one cultivates the ability to observe and reflect, ultimately guiding them toward decisions that resonate with their true selves.

One of the most significant long-term benefits of stillness is its ability to deepen our connection with nature. Individuals can cultivate presence and mindfulness through intentional silence and reflection in natural settings. Nature immersion promotes relaxation and nurtures a sense of belonging within the larger ecosystem. This connection encourages sustainable living practices as individuals become more aware of their environmental impact.

Over time, this awareness fosters a lifestyle aligned with ecological values, creating a feedback loop of gratitude and respect for the natural world.

Incorporating stillness into one's life also enhances the practice of gratitude. By embracing non-action moments, individuals can pause to appreciate the present, fostering a mindset of acceptance and contentment.

This aligns with the philosophy of amor fati, or love of fate, which encourages individuals to accept their circumstances and find beauty in life's unpredictability.

Over time, cultivating gratitude through stillness can transform one's perspective, leading to more excellent emotional stability and an overall sense of well-being. Individuals become more adept at recognizing the good in their lives, even amid challenges, which can lead to more fulfilling relationships and experiences.

Another significant benefit of the practice of stillness is applying wuwei or effortless action. By learning to navigate life with a mindset of non-resistance, individuals become more attuned to the flow of events, allowing them to respond thoughtfully rather than impulsively.

This approach not only reduces stress but also encourages a more balanced existence. Over time, as individuals practice stillness, they find themselves making choices more aligned with their core values, leading to a more authentic and purposeful life.

Finally, the long-term benefits of stillness extend to mental health and well-being. Disconnecting through stillness can lead to a slower, more meaningful life in a society increasingly dominated by digital distractions.

This digital detox, combined with intentional living, allows individuals to regain control over their attention and focus. As they cultivate stillness, they may experience decreased anxiety and improved emotional regulation.

Over time, this commitment to a quieter, more reflective way of living fosters resilience, enhancing one's ability to face challenges gracefully and composure. Ultimately, the long-term benefits of stillness create a foundation for a balanced and fulfilling life.

Chapter 10

Embracing Impermanence and Change

The Impermanence of All Things and Its Connection to Stillness

Getting caught up in the illusion of permanence in a world in constant flux is easy. We often find ourselves clinging to the past or anxiously anticipating the future, losing sight of the present moment.

However, embracing the impermanence of all things, including our existence, is crucial to cultivating a sense of presence and acceptance.

This concept is deeply rooted in the idea that change is an inherent and integral part of the human experience. It allows us to flow with it rather than resist it and navigate life's challenges with greater ease and stability.

By embracing impermanence, we acknowledge that everything is interconnected and interdependent and that our existence is a mere moment in the grand tapestry of time.

In embracing impermanence, we learn to observe our thoughts, emotions, and experiences without judgment, allowing us to transcend the limitations of the past and the uncertainty of the future.

This perspective fosters a sense of acceptance, not resignation, but a deep understanding that everything is constantly changing.
As we cultivate this awareness, we see the world with fresh eyes.

We notice the impermanence of the natural world, the cyclical nature of life and death, and the ever-changing landscape of our own lives. In this context, we understand that impermanence is not a source of fear but rather a reminder of the preciousness and fragility of existence.
By embracing the impermanence of all things, we open ourselves to the possibility of living more fully in the present.

We learn to cherish each moment, appreciate life's beauty, and find peace in change. As we surrender to the impermanence of everything, we discover freedom, not from life's challenges but from the burdens of attachment and expectation.

In the present moment, we find the space to breathe, be, and exist, free from the weights of the past and the uncertainties of the future.

In this state, we find a calm presence that allows us to navigate life's challenges with greater ease and poise. We learn to observe our thoughts, emotions, and experiences without judgment and to find peace during change.

This perspective enables us to transcend the limitations of the past and the uncertainty of the future and find a deeper connection to ourselves and the world around us.

By embracing impermanence, we understand that everything is constantly changing and that our existence is a mere moment in the grand tapestry of time. We learn to cherish each moment, appreciate the beauty of life, and find peace during change. In this context, we see a sense of freedom, not from life's challenges but from the burdens of attachment and expectation.

This perspective allows us to find peace amid change and to navigate life's challenges with greater ease and calmness. We learn to observe our thoughts, emotions, and experiences without judgment and find a deeper connection to ourselves and the world around us. In this state, we see a calm presence that allows us to live more fully in the present and find peace amid impermanence.

Ultimately, embracing impermanence is a path toward greater awareness and understanding of ourselves and the world. By letting go of attachment to the past and future, we create space to immerse ourselves fully in the present moment. We find peace, calm, and connection to ourselves and the world in this state.

As we navigate the complexities of life, embracing impermanence allows us to find a sense of freedom and peace. We learn to observe our thoughts, emotions, and experiences without judgment and find a deeper connection to ourselves and the world around us.

In this state, we see a calm presence that allows us to live more fully in the present and find peace amid impermanence. The impermanence of all things reminds us of the preciousness and fragility of existence. It is a call to live more fully in the present, to cherish each moment, and to find peace during change.

By embracing impermanence, we open ourselves to a deeper understanding of ourselves and the world around us and a greater sense of connection to all things.

Ultimately, embracing impermanence leads to greater awareness, understanding, and peace. It allows us to find a calm presence during change and to live more fully in the present. By letting go of attachment to the past and future, we create space to fully immerse ourselves in the present moment and find peace amid impermanence.

Embracing impermanence is a path toward greater awareness, understanding, and peace. It allows us to find a calm presence during change and to live more fully in the present. By letting go of attachment to the past and future, we create space to fully immerse ourselves in the present moment and find peace amid impermanence.

The Importance of Embracing Change and Uncertainty

Embracing change and uncertainty allows for personal growth and adaptability. In a world where nothing is permanent, letting go of the need for control and stability is essential. This mindset shift opens the door to new possibilities and allows us to face the unknown with an open mind. By doing so, we can discover hidden talents and strengths we never knew we had.

Appreciating the present moment and the beauty in change cultivates a more profound sense of fulfillment. When we focus on the present, we can see the opportunities with uncertainty. This mindset helps us view obstacles as opportunities for growth and transformation, increasing our resilience and ability to adapt.

Change and uncertainty are inevitable in life. Resisting them can lead to frustration and stagnation while embracing them can lead to personal growth and development. Uncertainty can be an opportunity for self-discovery, and embracing the impermanence of life fosters gratitude.

Adapting to challenges with a positive mindset is empowering. It allows us to approach difficulties confidently and creatively rather than fear and anxiety. By embracing change and uncertainty, we can develop a more optimistic outlook on life and become more resilient in adversity.

Incorporating mindfulness and self-reflection into our daily lives can help us develop a more positive relationship with change and uncertainty. Being present at the moment and focusing on our thoughts and emotions can create a greater sense of self-awareness and resilience.

Ultimately, embracing change and uncertainty allows us to live more authentically and intentionally. It encourages us to take risks, try new things, and push beyond our comfort zones. Doing so will enable us to develop a more profound sense of purpose and fulfillment and live a more meaningful and satisfying life.

The Role of Mindfulness in Navigating Transition and Change

Cultivating acceptance of impermanence is crucial to navigating life's transitions and changes. Recognizing that change is a natural part of life enables us to adapt quickly and openly. This mindset allows us to approach uncertainty with curiosity and wonder rather than resistance.

Mindfulness plays a significant role in navigating transition and change. We can respond to challenges with clarity and compassion by staying grounded and present in the moment. This involves awareness of our thoughts, emotions, and physical sensations without becoming overly identified.

Attuning to the cyclical nature of life's rhythms can also foster a sense of patience and trust in the process. As the seasons come and go, so do different periods in our lives.

By understanding and embracing this ebb and flow, we can learn to ride the waves of change more quickly. When faced with uncertainty, it's essential to prioritize self-care. Tending to our physical, emotional, and spiritual well-being provides the resilience to navigate challenging shifts gracefully.

This might involve engaging in activities that promote relaxation and stress reduction, such as meditation or yoga. Practicing non-attachment to outcomes is also vital in navigating change.

By letting go of rigid expectations, we can be more responsive to the unfolding present rather than resisting the natural flow of life. This involves cultivating a sense of flexibility and adaptability and being open to new possibilities and experiences.

By recognizing that change is inevitable, we can approach uncertainty with curiosity and wonder rather than fear and resistance. This mindset can transform our experience of change, allowing us to navigate even the most challenging transitions with greater ease and openness.

As we cultivate acceptance of impermanence, we can also learn to appreciate the present moment rather than getting caught up in worries about the future or regrets about the past. Being more fully present allows us to experience greater joy, peace, and fulfillment.

By embracing impermanence, we can learn to appreciate the beauty of life's uncertainties and approach challenges with curiosity and wonder. By cultivating mindfulness, acceptance, and self-care, we can learn to navigate life's transitions with greater ease and openness and live more fully and authentically in the present moment.

As we navigate life's transitions, it's essential to prioritize self-care and cultivate a sense of flexibility and adaptability. By doing so, we can learn to respond to challenges with greater clarity and compassion and to navigate even the most challenging transitions with greater ease and openness.

Cultivating acceptance of impermanence requires a willingness to relinquish our attachments to specific outcomes and trust in life's natural flow. By doing so, we can learn to navigate even the most challenging transitions with greater ease and openness and live more fully and authentically in the present moment.

By recognizing that change is inevitable, we can approach uncertainty with curiosity and wonder rather than fear and resistance. This mindset can transform our experience of change, allowing us to navigate even the most challenging transitions with greater ease and openness.

By embracing impermanence, we can learn to appreciate the present moment rather than getting caught up in worries about the future or regrets about the past. Being more fully present allows us to experience greater joy, peace, and fulfillment.

Cultivating acceptance of impermanence can also help us approach challenges with a sense of curiosity and wonder rather than fear and resistance. By embracing the natural flow of life, we can learn to navigate even the most challenging transitions with greater ease and openness and live more fully and authentically in the present moment.

As we cultivate acceptance of impermanence, we can also learn to appreciate the present moment rather than getting caught up in worries about the future or regrets about the past. Being more fully present allows us to experience greater joy, peace, and fulfillment.

By embracing impermanence, we can learn to appreciate the beauty of life's uncertainties and approach challenges with curiosity and wonder.

By cultivating mindfulness, acceptance, and self-care, we can learn to navigate life's transitions with greater ease and openness and live more fully and authentically in the present moment.

As we navigate life's transitions, it's essential to prioritize self-care and cultivate a sense of flexibility and adaptability. By doing so, we can learn to respond to challenges with greater clarity and compassion and to navigate even the most challenging transitions with greater ease and openness.

Cultivating acceptance of impermanence requires a willingness to relinquish our attachments to specific outcomes and trust in life's natural flow. By doing so, we can learn to navigate even the most challenging transitions with greater ease and openness and live more fully and authentically in the present moment.

The Connection Between Impermanence and Acceptance

Impermanence is a fundamental aspect of the universe, and understanding the transient nature of all things can foster acceptance. This acceptance can lead to a sense of peace, as letting go of attachment to fixed outcomes promotes mental and emotional well-being.

Impermanence teaches us to cherish the present moment, as appreciating the fleeting nature of experiences heightens our awareness and gratitude.

Change is a natural process, and resisting it can lead to anxiety and frustration. By embracing change, we can become more flexible and adaptable.

This allows us to navigate life's challenges more easily and find opportunities for growth and transformation. Accepting change enables us to view life's ebbs and flows as opportunities for evolution, which cultivates resilience.

In many Eastern philosophies, impermanence is seen as a fundamental principle of the universe. The concept of impermanence is closely tied to the idea of non-attachment.

Non-attachment allows us to let go of our attachment to specific outcomes and instead focus on the present moment. This can lead to a greater sense of peace and contentment.

The practice of mindfulness can also help us cultivate acceptance of impermanence. Mindfulness involves paying attention to the present moment without judgment or attachment. By practicing mindfulness, we can develop a greater awareness of the fleeting nature of experiences and learn to cherish the present moment.

Accepting change and letting go of attachment to fixed outcomes can help us find peace and contentment in the present moment. This allows us to navigate life's challenges more easily and find opportunities for growth and transformation. By embracing impermanence, we can cultivate a greater sense of peace and contentment and live more intentionally and meaningfully.

In uncertainty and change, it's essential to cultivate a sense of acceptance and let go of attachment to specific outcomes. By doing so, we can find peace and contentment in the present moment. Impermanence is a natural part of life; embracing it allows us greater freedom and flexibility.

Accepting impermanence can also lead to personal growth and transformation. We can cultivate resilience and find greater freedom and flexibility by viewing life's ebbs and flows as opportunities for evolution.

This allows us to navigate life's challenges more easily and find peace and contentment in the present moment.

Impermanence is a fundamental aspect of the universe, and understanding the transient nature of all things can foster acceptance. By embracing change and cultivating non-attachment, we can find peace and contentment. Impermanence teaches us to cherish the present moment and appreciate the fleeting nature of experiences.

During change and uncertainty, it's essential to cultivate a sense of acceptance and let go of attachment to specific outcomes. By doing so, we can find peace and contentment in the present moment.

Impermanence is a natural part of life; embracing it allows us greater freedom and flexibility. Accepting impermanence can also lead to tremendous gratitude and appreciation for the present moment. By cherishing the fleeting nature of experiences, we can develop a greater awareness of the beauty and wonder of life.

This allows us to find peace and contentment in the present moment and navigate life's challenges more easily. Impermanence is a fundamental aspect of the universe, and understanding the transient nature of all things can foster acceptance.

By embracing change and cultivating non-attachment, we can find peace and contentment. Impermanence teaches us to cherish the present moment and appreciate the fleeting nature of experiences.

Accepting impermanence can also lead to a greater sense of peace and contentment. We can find greater peace and happiness by letting go of attachment to specific outcomes and focusing on the present moment.

This allows us to navigate life's challenges more easily and find opportunities for growth and transformation.

Amid uncertainty and change, it's essential to cultivate a sense of acceptance and let go of attachment to specific outcomes. By doing so, we can find peace and contentment in the present moment. Impermanence is a natural part of life; embracing it allows us greater freedom and flexibility.

Accepting impermanence can also lead to personal growth and transformation. We can cultivate resilience and find greater freedom and flexibility by viewing life's ebbs and flows as opportunities for evolution. This allows us to navigate life's challenges more easily and find peace and contentment in the present moment.

Finding Freedom in the Face of Change

Cultivating an acceptance mindset is essential for living a fulfilling life. When we accept that change is a natural part of life, we let go of attachment and fear, allowing us to move forward efficiently. This mindset frees us from the need to control outcomes, enabling us to flow with the current of life.

Change can be challenging but also presents opportunities for growth and self-discovery. Reframing challenges as opportunities can unlock new perspectives and develop a more adaptive approach to life. This mindset allows us to see difficulties as chances to learn and evolve rather than as obstacles to be overcome.

Practicing non-resistance is a key aspect of cultivating acceptance. When we let go of the need to control outcomes, we can focus on the present moment and respond to situations more easily. This approach enables us to easily navigate life's transitions and milestones, celebrating the ebb and flow of life's journey.

One way to cultivate acceptance is to practice mindfulness and meditation. These practices help us stay present and focused, allowing us to navigate life's challenges easily.

Regular meditation practice can help us develop a greater sense of inner peace and calm, enabling us to respond to situations with greater clarity and wisdom.

In addition to mindfulness and meditation, we can cultivate acceptance by practicing gratitude. Focusing on the present moment and what we are thankful for can help us develop a greater appreciation and contentment.

This mindset allows us to see the beauty in life's transitions and milestones rather than viewing them as sources of stress and anxiety.

Cultivating a mindset of acceptance takes time and practice, but it is a valuable skill that can bring numerous benefits to our lives. By letting go of attachment and fear, we can live more freely and fully, embracing life's changes and challenges.

As we cultivate acceptance, we can develop a greater sense of inner peace and calm, enabling us to navigate life's journey with greater ease and clarity.

By practicing acceptance, we can develop greater self-awareness and compassion, allowing us to treat ourselves and others with incredible kindness and understanding.

This mindset enables us to live more harmoniously with ourselves and others, cultivating peace and contentment that permeates our lives.

In the end, cultivating an acceptance mindset is a journey that requires patience, practice, and dedication. However, the rewards are worth the effort as we develop greater self-awareness, compassion, and inner peace.

By embracing life's changes and challenges, we can live more freely and fully, cultivating a sense of acceptance and inner peace that brings joy and fulfillment.

Recognizing that impermanence is a natural part of life allows us to let go of our attachment to specific outcomes and instead focus on the present moment. This mindset enables us to find freedom in the face of change rather than feeling trapped or limited.

As we cultivate acceptance, we see challenges as opportunities for growth and self-discovery. This mindset allows us to reframe our perspective and approach life's difficulties with curiosity and openness. Doing so can unlock new perspectives and develop a more adaptive approach to life.

Ultimately, cultivating a mindset of acceptance is a journey that requires patience, practice, and dedication.

However, the rewards are worth the effort as we develop greater self-awareness, compassion, and inner peace. By embracing life's changes and challenges, we can live more freely and fully, cultivating a sense of acceptance and inner peace that brings joy and fulfillment.

Chapter 11

Embracing the Journey

The Path to Balance and Presence

The concept of balance and presence is integral to achieving a harmonious life, especially for those who seek authenticity and deeper connections with themselves and the world around them. In our fast-paced society, the pursuit of balance often feels elusive, as distractions and obligations pull us in multiple directions.

By embracing the philosophy of non-action, or Wuwei, we can cultivate a state of being that prioritizes presence over busyness. This mindful approach invites us to slow down, assess our values, and create space for introspection, allowing a clearer understanding of what truly matters.

Nature immersion serves as a powerful conduit for achieving this balance. Spending time outdoors reconnects us with our natural environment and fosters a sense of presence that is often absent in our daily lives.

Nature's sights, sounds, and sensations can ground us, providing a backdrop for reflection and awareness. Engaging in activities like hiking, gardening, or observing the changing seasons encourages us to be fully present, reminding us of life's rhythms beyond our screens and schedules. This immersion becomes a practice of intentional living, guiding us to align our daily actions with our core values.

The practice of gratitude further enhances intentional living. Embracing an attitude of appreciation, or Amor Fati, allows us to accept our circumstances and find meaning in every experience.

This acceptance does not suggest passivity; instead, it empowers us to recognize the beauty of life's challenges and joys. By cultivating gratitude, we create space for balance as we learn to prioritize what nourishes our spirit and fosters a sense of fulfillment.

This mental shift encourages a more profound engagement with our surroundings, facilitating a life that resonates with our innermost beliefs and aspirations.

Digital detoxification is essential in our journey toward balance and presence. Taking deliberate breaks from digital devices can significantly enhance our well-being in a world dominated by technology and constant connectivity.

Disconnecting from social media and digital distractions allows us to reconnect with ourselves and our immediate environment. Limiting our exposure to digital noise creates opportunities for reflection and mindfulness, enabling us to engage more deeply with our physical surroundings and people.

This practice nurtures presence and supports sustainable living as we become more aware of the impact of our choices on the planet.

Ultimately, the intersection of Eastern philosophy and Western wellness practices offers a rich framework for cultivating balance and presence. By integrating concepts like Wuwei with contemporary approaches to well-being, we can develop a holistic understanding of how to navigate our lives.

This blend encourages us to embrace stillness, practice intentionality, and foster gratitude, all while maintaining a deep connection with nature. As we embark on this path, we discover that the journey toward balance is not about striving for perfection but rather about nurturing a state of being that allows us to experience life fully and authentically.

Overcoming Challenges in Non-Action

The concept of non-action often presents a significant challenge in pursuing a life marked by intentionality and alignment with personal values.

Many independent-minded individuals grapple with the notion that stillness can be an active choice rather than a passive state. This resistance may stem from societal conditioning that equates busyness with productivity and success.

By exploring the philosophy of non-action, particularly the Eastern principle of wuwei, individuals can better understand how embracing stillness can lead to a deeper connection with themselves and the world around them.

One of the core challenges faced in practicing non-action is the pervasive fear of stagnation. In a culture that idolizes constant movement and achievement, the idea of stepping back can provoke anxiety and self-doubt.

However, it is essential to recognize that non-action does not imply inaction. Instead, it provides the opportunity for reflection, allowing individuals to reassess their priorities and values.

Engaging with nature can serve as a powerful antidote to this fear. The natural world thrives in cycles of stillness and growth, reminding us of the importance of patience and timing.

Another significant hurdle is the temptation to fill silence with distractions, especially in an age dominated by digital connectivity. A digital detox offers a practical way to confront this challenge, inviting individuals to disconnect from the noise of modern life and engage with their surroundings.

Individuals can cultivate a sense of presence that fosters deeper insights and connections by intentionally setting aside time for stillness through meditation, nature walks, or sitting quietly. This practice enhances mindfulness and encourages gratitude for the simple moments that often go unnoticed.

Embracing non-action can also bring up guilt or inadequacy, particularly among those who equate worth with productivity. Overcoming this mindset requires a fundamental shift in the perception of value and success.

By adopting a framework of gratitude, individuals can learn to appreciate the value of being rather than doing. This perspective aligns closely with the philosophy of amor fati, or love of one's fate, which encourages accepting life's circumstances.

Through this lens, stillness becomes a powerful tool for personal growth, allowing individuals to cultivate resilience and adaptability in facing life's challenges.

Finally, integrating non-action principles into a sustainable lifestyle can be transformative. The intersection of stillness and sustainable living fosters a harmonious relationship with nature, emphasizing the importance of mindful consumption and ecological balance.

By recognizing the impact of their choices, individuals can align their actions with their values, creating a life that is fulfilling and respectful of the environment.

In this way, overcoming challenges in non-action becomes not just a personal journey but a collective movement toward a more intentional and harmonious existence.

Celebrating Progress and Growth

Celebrating progress and growth is essential to achieving balance through stillness. Recognizing our advancements can feel counterintuitive in a world that often prioritizes constant activity and productivity.

However, in these moments of reflection, we cultivate a deeper understanding of ourselves and our connection to the natural world. By embracing the philosophy of non-action, we learn to appreciate the subtle shifts in our lives, allowing us to celebrate the milestones that may otherwise go unnoticed in the hustle and bustle of daily existence.

Nature immersion serves as a powerful catalyst for recognizing growth. When we engage with the natural environment, we are reminded of the cycles of life, from the slow unfurling of a fern to the deliberate migration of birds.

Each season presents an opportunity to assess our progress, echoing nature's rhythms. As we pause to observe and appreciate these changes, we foster a sense of presence that helps us acknowledge our own journeys, no matter how small.

This connection encourages us to honor our narratives, understanding that growth can be gradual and often imperceptible, much like the subtle transformations around us.

Intentional living further enhances our ability to celebrate progress. We create a framework for acknowledging and appreciating growth by aligning our lives with personal values.

As we engage in practices that reflect our true selves, each step taken becomes a testament to our commitment to authenticity. This intentionality cultivates an environment where we can celebrate our achievements and the lessons learned from challenges faced along the way. In this way, every experience, whether perceived as positive or negative, contributes to our growth and deserves recognition.

Incorporating gratitude practices into our daily routines amplifies our ability to celebrate progress. By fostering acceptance through amor fati, or love of fate, we learn to embrace our life circumstances as integral to our growth.

This acceptance allows us to appreciate our journeys and recognize the value of triumphs and trials. Gratitude shifts our focus from what we lack to what we have achieved, fostering a mindset that celebrates incremental progress rather than an unattainable ideal. In this space of gratitude, we find the strength to acknowledge our growth authentically.

Finally, a digital detox can facilitate a clearer perspective on our progress. In an age dominated by constant connectivity, stepping back from technology allows us to reconnect with ourselves and the world.

As we unplug from distractions, we create space for introspection and mindfulness, enabling us to celebrate our growth without the noise of external expectations.

In this stillness, we can reflect on our journeys, recognizing the importance of each step taken and affirming our commitment to sustainable living and harmony with nature. By celebrating progress, we reinforce our connection to ourselves and our purpose, enriching our lives profoundly.

Chapter 12

Embodied Presence and Holistic Health

The Interconnectedness of Body, Mind, and Spirit

In the intricate dance between our physical and mental states, it's becoming increasingly clear that our bodily sensations, emotional experiences, and cognitive processes are deeply intertwined.

This complex web of relationships underscores the significance of embodied presence in maintaining overall well-being. As we navigate the complexities of modern life, it's essential to recognize the profound impact that our physical and emotional experiences have on our mental clarity, cognitive function, and overall health.

Scientific evidence is mounting, demonstrating that embodied practices such as meditation and yoga can profoundly impact our physiological state, reducing stress levels, lowering blood pressure, and boosting immune function. By cultivating bodily awareness, we can experience these benefits firsthand, improving overall health and quality of life.

This section will delve into the transformative power of embodied presence, exploring its role in facilitating natural healing processes, promoting overall well-being, and fostering self-awareness.

We'll examine how embodied practices can reshape our brains and improve focus, emotional regulation, and cognitive function. By understanding the intricate web of relationships between our physical, emotional, and spiritual selves, we can tap into our innate capacity for self-healing and cultivate a more profound connection to ourselves and the world around us.

Through scientific research, personal anecdotes, and practical tips, we'll explore the many benefits of embodied presence, from improved mental clarity and emotional regulation to increased self-awareness and a more profound sense of connection to our bodies and the world around us.
By incorporating embodied practices into our daily routine and cultivating bodily awareness, we can experience the transformative power of embodied presence firsthand, leading to a more fulfilling, intentional life.

The Science Behind the Benefits of Embodied Presence

The mind-body connection is a well-established concept in scientific research. It demonstrates the intricate link between our physical and mental states.

Studies have shown that our bodily sensations, emotional experiences, and cognitive processes are profoundly interconnected and influence one another in complex ways.

This intricate web of relationships underscores the significance of embodied presence in maintaining overall well-being.

Research has consistently shown that embodied practices, such as meditation and yoga, profoundly impact our physiological state.

Regular practice has been linked to reduced stress levels, lower blood pressure, and boosted immune function. By cultivating bodily awareness, we can experience these benefits firsthand, improving overall health and quality of life.

The neurological impacts of embodied practices are equally compelling. Meditation, in particular, has been shown to reshape the brain's structure and function, improving focus, emotional regulation, and cognitive function.

This neural reorganization can enhance mental clarity, improve decision-making, and increase resilience when facing challenges. The mind-body-spirit connection plays a crucial role in facilitating natural healing processes.

By acknowledging the interconnectedness of our physical, emotional, and spiritual selves, we can tap into our innate capacity for self-healing. This holistic approach to health recognizes that our well-being is not solely the domain of external medical interventions but an embodied experience that requires conscious attention and care.

Cultivating bodily awareness is a key component of this approach. Tuning into our physical sensations, emotions, and thoughts can help us better understand ourselves and our place in the world.

This increased self-awareness can lead to greater self-acceptance, allowing us to release judgment and self-criticism and cultivate compassion and kindness toward ourselves.

Practically, this means incorporating embodied practices into our daily routine, such as mindfulness meditation, yoga, or simply paying attention to our physical sensations and emotions.

By doing so, we can experience the transformative power of embodied presence firsthand, leading to improved overall well-being and a deeper connection to ourselves and the world around us.

In addition to its physical and emotional benefits, cultivating bodily awareness can profoundly impact mental clarity and cognitive function. We can access new levels of creativity, problem-solving, and innovative thinking by quieting the mind and tuning into our bodily sensations.

This, in turn, can lead to tremendous success and fulfillment in our personal and professional lives.

As we navigate the complexities of modern life, it's essential to recognize the significance of embodied presence in maintaining our overall well-being. By acknowledging the intricate web of relationships between our physical, emotional, and spiritual selves, we can tap into our innate capacity for self-healing and cultivate a more profound connection to ourselves and the world around us.

By incorporating embodied practices into our daily routine and cultivating bodily awareness, we can experience the transformative power of embodied presence firsthand. This, in turn, can lead to improved overall health, greater mental clarity, and a more profound sense of connection to ourselves and the world around us.

The mind-body connection is a complex and multifaceted concept, and much is still to be learned about its intricacies. However, one thing is clear: embodied presence is key to unlocking our full potential and living a more fulfilling, intentional life.

By embracing the transformative power of embodied presence, we can experience its many benefits and cultivate a more profound connection to ourselves and the world around us.

In a world constantly bombarded with distractions and stimuli, losing touch with our bodily sensations and emotions is easy. However, we can regain balance and harmony by consciously tuning into our physical and emotional experiences.

By prioritizing embodied presence and cultivating bodily awareness, we can develop self-awareness, self-acceptance, and self-compassion. This, in turn, can lead to greater resilience, better decision-making, and a more profound sense of connection to ourselves and the world around us.

Ultimately, the benefits of embodied presence are far-reaching and multifaceted. By embracing this approach to health and well-being, we can experience a profound sense of transformation and growth, leading to a more fulfilling, intentional life.

This complex interplay between our physical, emotional, and spiritual selves requires a holistic approach to health and wellness. By acknowledging the intricate web of relationships between these different aspects of our being, we can tap into our innate capacity for self-healing and cultivate a more profound connection to ourselves and the world around us.

By incorporating embodied practices into our daily routine and cultivating bodily awareness, we can experience the transformative power of embodied presence firsthand. This, in turn, can lead to improved overall health, greater mental clarity, and a more profound sense of connection to ourselves and the world around us.

Cultivating bodily awareness is a key component of this approach. Tuning into our physical sensations, emotions, and thoughts can help us better understand ourselves and our place in the world.

This increased self-awareness can lead to greater self-acceptance, allowing us to release judgment and self-criticism and instead cultivate compassion and kindness toward ourselves.

Incorporating embodied practices into our daily routine can profoundly impact our overall well-being. By consciously tuning into our physical and emotional experiences, we can experience a sense of balance and harmony in our lives.

The mind-body connection is a complex and multifaceted concept, and much is still to be learned about its intricacies. However, one thing is clear: embodied presence is key to unlocking our full potential and living a more fulfilling, intentional life.

By embracing the transformative power of embodied presence, we can experience its many benefits and cultivate a more profound connection to ourselves and the world around us.

By prioritizing embodied presence and cultivating bodily awareness, we can develop self-awareness, self-acceptance, and self-compassion. This, in turn, can lead to greater resilience, better decision-making, and a more profound sense of connection to ourselves and the world around us.

The benefits of embodied presence are far-reaching and multifaceted. By embracing this approach to health and wellness, we can experience a profound sense of transformation and growth, leading to a more fulfilling, intentional life.

Ultimately, it's essential to recognize the significance of embodied presence in maintaining our overall well-being. By acknowledging the intricate web of relationships between our physical, emotional, and spiritual selves, we can tap into our innate capacity for self-healing and cultivate a more profound connection to ourselves and the world around us.

By incorporating embodied practices into our daily routine and cultivating bodily awareness, we can experience the transformative power of embodied presence firsthand.

This, in turn, can lead to improved overall health, greater mental clarity, and a more profound sense of connection to ourselves and the world around us.

Cultivating bodily awareness is a key component of this approach. Tuning into our physical sensations, emotions, and thoughts can help us better understand ourselves and our place in the world.

This increased self-awareness can lead to greater self-acceptance, allowing us to release judgment and self-criticism and cultivate compassion and kindness toward ourselves.

The Connection Between Embodied Presence and Self-Awareness

Embodied presence is a state of being that cultivates self-awareness by tuning into the physical, mental, and emotional aspects of one's experience. By acknowledging and accepting one's body, mind, and spirit, individuals can better understand themselves and their place in the world.

One key benefit of embodied presence is that it allows individuals to connect with their inner experience without judgment. This means observing thoughts and emotions without attachment or aversion and cultivating a sense of curiosity and compassion.

By doing so, individuals can develop greater emotional intelligence, which is essential for making intentional choices and living a life that is authentic to who they are.

Embodied presence also enables individuals to live in alignment with their values and goals. When we are present in our bodies, we are more attuned to our physical needs and desires and better able to listen to our inner wisdom.

This allows us to make choices that align with our values and goals rather than being driven by external pressures or expectations.

In addition to these benefits, embodied presence can lead to greater self-knowledge and presence. Tuning into our physical sensations, movements, and rhythms can help us better understand ourselves and our place in the world. This can lead to greater confidence, creativity, and joy as we engage more fully.

One way to cultivate embodied presence is through mindfulness practices such as yoga, tai chi, or simply paying attention to our breath. By slowing down and focusing on our physical experience, we can develop a greater sense of awareness and connection to our bodies.

This can be especially beneficial in today's fast-paced world, where we are often encouraged to push ourselves to be more productive and efficient.

As we cultivate embodied presence, we can begin to integrate the different aspects of ourselves, including body, mind, and spirit. This can lead to a more holistic and centered state of being, where we feel more grounded and connected to ourselves and the world around us.

We can develop self-awareness, emotional intelligence, and intentional living by embracing embodied presence. Slowing down and focusing on our physical experience can help us develop greater awareness and connection to our bodies.

This can lead to greater confidence, creativity, and joy as we engage more fully.

As we cultivate embodied presence, we can see the world in a new light. We can see the beauty and wonder of the present moment and feel more connected to ourselves and the world. This can lead to greater peace, joy, and fulfillment.

In time, embodied presence can become a natural state of being fully engaged in our lives and more connected to ourselves and the world around us. By embracing this way of being, we can develop greater self-awareness, emotional intelligence, and intentional living, leading to a more authentic and fulfilling life.

By cultivating embodied presence, we can connect better to our bodies and inner wisdom. This can lead to greater self-awareness, emotional intelligence, and intentional living. By embracing this practice, we can live a more authentic and fulfilling life and cultivate greater peace, joy, and fulfillment.

Cultivating embodied presence can help us develop self-awareness, emotional intelligence, and intentional living. Slowing down and focusing on our physical experience can help us create greater awareness and connection to our bodies.

This can lead to greater confidence, creativity, and joy as we engage more fully. We can see the world in a new light as we cultivate embodied presence. We can see the beauty and wonder of the present moment and feel more connected to ourselves and the world.

This can lead to greater peace, joy, and fulfillment as we are more fully engaged and connected to ourselves and the world. We can develop self-awareness, emotional intelligence, and intentional living by embracing embodied presence.

Slowing down and focusing on our physical experience can also help us become more aware of and connected to our bodies. This can lead to greater confidence, creativity, and joy as we are more fully engaged. In time, embodied presence can become a natural state of being, allowing us to be fully engaged in our lives and more connected to ourselves and the world around us.

By embracing this way of being, we can develop greater self-awareness, emotional intelligence, and intentional living, leading to a more authentic and fulfilling life.

By cultivating embodied presence, we can connect better to our bodies and inner wisdom. This can lead to greater self-awareness, emotional intelligence, and intentional living.

By embracing this practice, we can live a more authentic and fulfilling life and cultivate greater peace, joy, and fulfillment.

Cultivating embodied presence can help us develop self-awareness, emotional intelligence, and intentional living. Slowing down and focusing on our physical experience can also help us create greater awareness and connection to our bodies.

This can lead to greater confidence, creativity, and joy as we engage more fully.

As we continue cultivating embodied presence, we can see the world in a new light, experience the beauty and wonder of the present moment, and feel more connected to ourselves and the world around us.

This can lead to greater peace, joy, and fulfillment as we are more fully engaged and connected to ourselves and the world. We can develop self-awareness, emotional intelligence, and intentional living by embracing embodied presence.

Slowing down and focusing on our physical experience can also help us become more aware and connected to our bodies. This can lead to greater confidence, creativity, and joy as we engage more fully.

The Importance of Self-Care and Self-Compassion

Self-care is essential for maintaining holistic health. It nourishes the body, mind, and spirit, promoting overall well-being.

Self-compassion is a vital component of self-care. Treating oneself with kindness, understanding, and acceptance helps mitigate stress and cultivate inner peace.

Sustainable self-care routines empower individuals to navigate life's challenges with resilience, enhance emotional regulation, improve physical health, and foster a sense of balance.

Mindfulness-based self-care techniques, such as meditation, breathwork, and sensory awareness, deepen the mind-body-spirit connection and aid in achieving a state of present-moment awareness.

Engaging in creative self-expression is a form of holistic self-care, as exploring artistic pursuits can tap into one's innate creativity, fostering personal growth and emotional fulfillment.

Artists, writers, and musicians often report increased self-awareness and emotional intelligence through their creative endeavors.

Practicing self-compassion and self-care can profoundly impact one's overall well-being. Treating ourselves with kindness and understanding makes us better equipped to handle life's challenges and setbacks. This can lead to increased resilience, improved physical health, and a greater sense of balance in life.

One key benefit of self-care is its ability to reduce stress and anxiety. When prioritizing self-care, we can better manage our stress levels and cultivate inner peace.

This can lead to improved relationships, increased productivity, and greater well-being. Incorporating self-care into our daily routines can be as simple as taking a few minutes each day to practice deep breathing, meditation, or yoga.

It can also involve engaging in creative activities like painting, writing, or playing music. The key is to find activities that bring us joy and help us feel connected to our inner selves.

The benefits of self-care are numerous and can profoundly impact our overall well-being. By prioritizing self-care and practicing self-compassion, we can develop the resilience and emotional intelligence needed to navigate life's challenges easily and cultivate a greater inner peace.

In today's fast-paced world, it's easy to get caught up in the hustle and bustle and forget to take care of ourselves. However, self-care is not a luxury but necessary for maintaining holistic health and promoting overall well-being.

Self-care is a holistic approach to health that encompasses physical, emotional, and mental well-being. By prioritizing self-care and practicing self-compassion, we can develop the tools to navigate life's challenges easily and cultivate a greater sense of inner peace.

Ultimately, self-care is about cultivating a greater sense of self-awareness, emotional intelligence, and inner peace. By prioritizing self-care and practicing self-compassion, we can develop the resilience and emotional intelligence needed to navigate life's challenges easily and cultivate outstanding balance and well-being.

Through self-care, we can cultivate a greater sense of self-awareness, emotional intelligence, and inner peace. By prioritizing self-care and practicing self-compassion, we can develop the tools to navigate life's challenges easily and cultivate a greater sense of balance and well-being.

In today's world, it's essential to prioritize self-care and take care of ourselves. By doing so, we can develop the resilience and emotional intelligence needed to navigate life's challenges easily and cultivate a greater inner peace.

Self-care is not a one-size-fits-all approach. What works for one person may only work for one person. It's essential to experiment and find what works best for you.

Whether you meditate, do yoga, or simply walk in nature, the most important thing is finding activities that bring you joy and help you feel connected to your inner self.

Self-care can have a profound impact on our overall well-being. By prioritizing self-care and practicing self-compassion, we can develop the resilience and emotional intelligence needed to navigate life's challenges easily and cultivate a greater inner peace.

Incorporating self-care into our daily routines can be a powerful way to improve physical and emotional health. By caring for ourselves, we can develop the tools needed to navigate life's challenges easily and cultivate a greater sense of balance and well-being.

Self-care is essential for maintaining holistic health and promoting overall well-being. By prioritizing self-care and practicing self-compassion, we can develop the resilience and emotional intelligence needed to navigate life's challenges easily and cultivate a greater inner peace.

Self-care is essential for maintaining holistic health and promoting overall well-being. By prioritizing self-care and practicing self-compassion, we can develop the resilience and emotional intelligence needed to navigate life's challenges easily and cultivate a greater inner peace.

Conclusion

In Summary of "The Power of Stillness: Finding Balance Through Non-Action

This book explores the transformative concept of stillness, positioning it as a vital antidote to the constant noise and myriad distractions that characterize modern life.

The introduction sets the stage by acknowledging individuals' profound challenges in maintaining balance amidst the rapid pace of contemporary existence. It emphasizes the necessity of embracing non-action—a practice that fosters mindfulness and allows for the genuine expression of one's true self.

Chapter 1 serves as a foundational exploration of the essence of stillness. It sheds light on the alarming decline of stillness in our current society, attributing this shift to the demands of technology and a culture that often glorifies busyness.

The chapter advocates for the deliberate integration of stillness into our daily lives, illustrating its critical role in enhancing overall well-being. It underscores the interconnection between mind, body, and spirit, showing how cultivating stillness can lead to a more harmonious existence.

Chapter 2 shifts the focus to nature immersion, highlighting the profound healing power of the natural world. This chapter celebrates mindful practices—such as meditation in natural settings—that facilitate profound experiences of stillness.

Here, the philosophy of Wuwei, or non-action, is introduced. The idea is presented not as passivity but as an active embrace of spontaneity and flow, encouraging readers to relinquish the illusion of control in favor of a more organic engagement with life.

Chapter 3 delves into intentional living, examining how aligning one's actions with personal values enables a more meaningful and fulfilling existence. It touches on the practical applications of intentionality, urging readers to consider how their choices reflect their core beliefs and contribute to sustainable living.

Chapter 4 brings the significance of gratitude to the forefront. This chapter details the wide-ranging benefits of cultivating gratitude for mental and physical health and offers practical strategies for weaving gratitude practices into the fabric of daily life.

Readers are encouraged to reflect on the power of appreciation in fostering positive relationships and enhancing overall life satisfaction.

In Chapter 5, the book revisits the philosophy of non-action in greater depth. It provides a historical context for this philosophy, drawing connections between ancient wisdom and its relevance in the modern world. Readers are invited to reflect on how embracing non-action can lead to profound personal transformation.

Chapter 6 tackles the pressing issue of digital detoxification, addressing the pervasive impact of technology on mental health. It explores the addictive nature of digital devices and social media, urging readers to consider stepping back from screens to reclaim their mental and emotional well-being.

Chapter 7 outlines the fundamental principles of sustainable living, encouraging readers to harmonize their lifestyles with the rhythms of nature. It invites reflection on the choices one makes regarding consumption and waste, advocating for a lifestyle that respects and nurtures the planet.

In Chapter 8, the text draws bridges between Eastern philosophical traditions and Western wellness practices. This chapter emphasizes stillness's vital role in achieving holistic health, integrating insights from both traditions to present a unified approach to well-being.

Chapter 9 offers practical techniques for cultivating a personal practice of stillness. It shares various methods, such as meditation, breathwork, and mindful observation, illustrating the long-term benefits of integrating these practices into everyday life for a more profound sense of peace and clarity.

Chapter 10 dives into the themes of impermanence and change, focusing on the essential role of mindfulness in navigating life's transitions. It highlights the importance of embracing uncertainty and learning to find strength and resilience in the face of change.

Finally, Chapter 11 celebrates the ongoing journey toward balance and presence. It offers heartfelt encouragement to readers, inspiring them to persevere through challenges encountered while practicing non-action and cultivating stillness.

As we conclude our exploration into the transformative power of stillness, it becomes crucial to reflect on the profound insights we've gathered. In a world that often equates worth with unending action and productivity, we have unearthed the profound value of stepping back, embracing non-action, and fostering the art of being present.

Through a keener understanding of the essence of stillness, immersive experiences in nature, and a commitment to intentional living, we can reclaim our connection to ourselves and the world around us.

We have learned that stillness is not a void to be feared but a rich tapestry woven with potential for growth, reflection, and healing. It grants clarity in chaotic times, empowering us to align our lives with our deepest values and nurture meaningful relationships.

By integrating gratitude practices, engaging with the philosophy of non-action, and dedicating ourselves to a digital detox, we can cultivate a profound appreciation for life's fleeting moments. Embracing impermanence has illuminated the truth that liberation is found in our ability to accept the present moment and navigate change with grace.

Ultimately, the journey toward stillness is not a fixed endpoint but an ongoing process of self-discovery and renewal. As we continue to confront the complexities of modern existence, we carry forward the invaluable lessons of balance, presence, and intentional living, paving the way for a more fulfilling and authentic life.

In essence, this book extends an invitation to embrace the profound power of stillness in our everyday lives—not as an escape from the world but as a means to forge deeper connections, cultivate awareness, and engage fully with the life we live. As you set aside these pages, may you discover solace in the stillness that envelops you, guiding you toward a life that resonates with purpose and authenticity.

If you enjoyed this book and would like to read more from Faith Harmony
Other titles that you might enjoy.

Mind of Matter - a book discussing NLP and habit-changing

Mind of Matter guided meditations—This book contains guided meditations to help alter the mind from negativity to positivity.

Rising Higher is about shaping and molding yourself to be your best version.

Awakening the soul - is all about spiritual renewal for the stay-at-home mother.

Self-Love Rituals: Daily Self-Care for an Empowered Life - Breaking down actions to love yourself better.

"Beyond Etremes - Cognitive Behavioral Therapy For Balance Thinking" - helping anyone to overcome black-and-white thinking.

Printed in Great Britain
by Amazon